Look Smarter Than You Are with Smart View and Essbase 11

An End User's Guide

Edward Roske
Tracy McMullen

1st Edition

interRel Press, Arlington, Texas

Look Smarter Than You Are with Smart View and Essbase 11: An End User's Guide

Edward Roske
Tracy McMullen

Published by:

interRel Press
A Division of interRel Consulting Partners
Suite 304
1000 Ballpark Way
Arlington, TX 76011

Library of Congress Cataloging-in-Publication Data
Roske, Edward, McMullen, Tracy
         Look Smarter Than You Are with Smart View and Essbase 11: An End User's Guide

Edward Roske, Tracy McMullen 1st ed.
         p. 288 cm.
         Includes index.
         ISBN 978-0-557-06125-9

This book is dedicated to our families. To our children who gave up many hours of "mom" and "dad" time and to our loving spouses for their eternal patience.

Edward Roske, Tracy McMullen

ABOUT THE AUTHORS

Edward Roske fell in love with Hyperion at first sight. In 1995, Edward was working for the Moore Business Forms printing facility in Mundelein, Illinois. While his official title was "Coordinator of Finance", his role focused on coordinating the linking of many, many Microsoft Excel sheets. When someone in his area would delete a row in a supporting workbook and #REF errors would show up in the summary workbook, Edward personally tracked them down cell-by-cell. When he saw his first demonstration of Arbor Essbase (as it was known at the time), he quit his job to become a full-time Essbase consultant (becoming in the process one of those rare individuals who quit a stable job to consult on a product for which he had absolutely no experience).

Edward is a pioneer. He was one of the first Essbase Certified consultants in the world. He was also one of the first people in the world to become certified in Hyperion Planning. While at Moore, he also obtained his first patent proving that there are still new ideas waiting to be discovered and exploited for financial gain.

In May of 1997, Edward left his senior consulting position with a Chicago-based firm to co-found interRel Consulting along with Eduardo Quiroz. Proving that being humble will get you nowhere, Edward helped write interRel's original motto: "Reaching for perfection, we deliver the impossible in record time." He has been the CEO of interRel Consulting since its inception growing them to be a multi-million dollar firm with offices from coast-to-coast.

Edward still keeps his Essbase skills sharp. He has overseen successful Hyperion implementations at over 100 companies. His optimizations have resulted in Essbase calculation improvements of more than 99.99%.

Continuing his quest to become the world's foremost Essbase-evangelist, Edward has been a regular speaker at annual Hyperion user conferences since 1995 and he is noted for his humorous slant to technically boring information. He is the Essbase Domain Lead for the Oracle Applications Users Group (OAUG) and chair of the Hyperion track for the Oracle Developer Users Group's (ODTUG) annual Kaleidoscope conference. Recently, Oracle awarded him the title of "Oracle ACE Director." Visit Edward's blog at http://looksmarter.blogspot.com/.

Though not especially relevant, he also likes puppies.

ABOUT THE AUTHORS

Tracy McMullen, Oracle ACE Director, has been leading the development of Enterprise Performance Management and Data Warehousing applications for over 10 years. Roles on projects have ranged from developer, to architect and project manager on technologies from Hyperion and Business Objects to Cognos and Oracle. She's seen all of the business intelligence tools and Hyperion is her favorite.

Tracy started her career at Arthur Andersen Business Consulting on a project programming in RPG (fun stuff!). Thankfully, her next project introduced her to the world of multidimensional databases with a Cognos PowerPlay implementation for an oil and gas client (many years ago Tracy was certified in Cognos PowerPlay and Impromptu). Next, she helped clients from various industries revolutionize their information delivery with Hyperion and other technologies. After years of successful business intelligence implementations, a few shredded documents changed her career path from future Partner to eliminating cancer.

Tracy next joined The University of Texas M.D. Anderson Cancer Center where she lead the charge in implementing budget and planning solutions utilizing Hyperion Planning. Fate stepped in once again with relocation to the South Texas Coast and Tracy found her new home with interRel Consulting as Director of Special Projects (which really means she does a million different things from consulting to training to project management to sales).

Tracy is a Hyperion Certified Consultant for Hyperion Essbase, Hyperion Certified Solutions Architect for Hyperion Planning and a Certified Project Management Professional (PMP). Tracy has been a regular instructor at interRel, user conferences and other professional seminars since 2000 on topics including information delivery, business intelligence, data warehousing, and Hyperion implementations. Visit Tracy's blog at http://looksmarterthanyouare2.blogspot.com/. Her strong technical background is complimented by comprehensive practical experience in project management, a skill important not only on the job but at home as well where she manages her kids on a daily basis (ok, she attempts to manage with moderate success).

ABOUT INTERREL CONSULTING

Integrated solutions are key to providing our clients the timely information they need to make critical business decisions. Our philosophy, experience, and methodologies are integral components of our application development, project management, optimization and training. As a result of our experience and commitment to excellence, interRel has become one of the premier providers of analytical solutions using Oracle BI and Hyperion solutions.

interRel solves business problems through utilizing Business Intelligence (BI) and Enterprise Performance Management (EPM) technologies. Our EPM Assessment is designed to identify an organization's current EPM current state relative to the corporate strategy.

interRel has been in business since 1997, and we take pride in delivering our solutions with small teams composed of members with an average of over eight years of Oracle Hyperion and BI related tools, application and consulting experience.

Exclusive EPM/BI consultancy

- 100% of revenue is Oracle EPM / BI-Derived
- 100% of Consultants specialize in Oracle EPM System/Hyperion
- 100% of Senior Consultants are Hyperion Certified
- Senior Consultants have 8+ years of experience
- Junior Consultants have 5+ years of experience

Oracle Hyperion Community - Training, Free Webcasts, and More

Through our various outlets, our focus is always to interact and help others in the Oracle Hyperion community.

If you like this book, join us in person for a hands-on training class. interRel Consulting offers classroom education on a full spectrum of Oracle EPM solutions, including standard course offerings such as *Essbase and Planning Accelerated Fundamentals*, tailored for new Administrators as well as unique advanced courses like *Hyperion Calc Scripts for Mere Mortals*. All classes are taught by knowledgeable, certified trainers whose experience combines to an average of 8+ years. This interactive environment allows attendees the opportunity to master the skill set needed to implement, develop and manage Hyperion solutions successfully. All classes are held at headquarters in Dallas and offer CPE accreditation. interRel Consulting also provides custom training to clients.

interRel Consulting proudly offers free weekly webcasts. These webcasts include the full scope of Oracle BI and EPM System (Hyperion) products, including Essbase, Planning & HFM. Webcasts are primarily held every non-holiday week and twice in most weeks. Topics include 'Tips, Tricks & Best Practices,' which gives you an insider's guide to optimize the usage of your solution. The 'Administration' series focuses on making your job easier and giving a snapshot of the Accelerated Fundamentals course outline while the 'Overview' webcasts discuss the highlights of a solution and how it can be used effectively. All webcasts include interactive examples and demonstrations to see how the products really work.

Awards & Recognitions

- 2008 Oracle Titan Award winner for "EPM Solution" of the year
- 2008 Oracle Excellence Award winner with Pearson Education
- One of the fastest growing companies in USA (Inc. Magazine, '08)
- The only company in the world *of any kind* with two Oracle ACE Directors and one Oracle ACE

interRel's commitment to providing our customers with unsurpassed customer service and unmatched expertise make interRel the partner of choice for a large number of companies across the world. Learn more at www.interrel.com.

ACKNOWLEDGEMENTS

If we were to thank all of those who assisted us in the creation of this book, we would have to not only personally mention hundreds of people but also several companies and one or two federal agencies (though we will give a special shout-out to those wacky guys over at the Internal Revenue Service: keep it real, yo!). Suffice to say, if this book stands tall, it is only by balancing on the heads of giants.

Those contributing significant content to this book include Eduardo "Short Stack" Quiroz and John "Grumpy Smurf" Scott, though most of their actual submissions were later removed due to incorrectness, decency laws and the unanimous decision by the authors that delivery of technical information in sonata verse, though revolutionary, would not be acceptable to the audience of this book. Thanks also to Kelli Stein, Lisa DeJohn, Christopher "CTI" Solomon, Debbie Riter, Josie Manzano, and Robin Banks.

Thank you to Laura Gregor, Jane Arrington, Donna Garner, and Steve Press for being long-time, strong supporters. We would like to thank some of the product folks at Oracle for their insight and advice: thanks to Shubhomoy Bhattacharya, Guillaume Arnaud, Shankar Viswanathan, Al Marciante, Aneel Shenker, John O'Rourke, Rich Clayton, and Mike Nader.

A special thank you is extended to John Kopcke for agreeing to write our foreword of Look Smarter Than You Are with Essbase.

Edward also wants to say "thank you" to Melissa Vorhies Roske, Vanessa Roske, and Eliot Roske for giving up their time with him on evenings and weekends, so he could make his publishing deadline. On a related note, Edward would also like to thank in advance anyone who can figure out a way to get rid of publishing deadlines.

Tracy McMullen would like to thank Blanche and Randy McMullen Sr. for babysitting so that she could write a large portion of this book. Thanks to mom and dad, Dot and Bob Collins, for their never-ending support and Randy, Taylor and Reese for their patience and understanding.

We give our sincerest gratitude to all the people above, and we hope that they feel that this book is partly theirs as well (just without the fame, glory and most importantly, the royalties).

DISCLAIMER

This book is designed to provide supporting information about the related subject matter. It is being sold to you and/or your company with the understanding that the author and the publisher are not engaged by you to provide legal, accounting, or any other professional services of any kind. If assistance is required (legal, expert, or otherwise), seek out the services of a competent professional such as a consultant.

It is not the purpose of this book to reprint all of the information that is already available on the subject at hand. The purpose of this book is to complement and supplement other texts already available to you. For more information (especially including technical reference information), please contact the software vendor directly or use your on-line help.

Great effort has been made to make this book as complete and accurate as possible. That said, there may be errors both typographic and in content. As such, use this book only as a general guide and not as the ultimate source for specific information on the software product. Further, this book contains information on the software that was generally available as of the publishing date.

The purpose of this book is to entertain while educating. The author and interRel Press shall have neither liability nor responsibility to any person living or dead or entity currently or previously in existence with respect to any loss or damage caused or alleged to be caused directly, indirectly, or otherwise by the information contained in this book.

If you do not wish to abide by all parts of the above disclaimer, please stop reading now and return this book to the publisher for a full refund.

TABLE OF CONTENTS

Chapter 1:
How I Almost Killed a Man

In the worst of times, desperate men can be driven to commit acts of madness. Case in point, I'm sitting in my cubicle at this moment, trying to figure out how to kill my boss with only the power of my thoughts. I've come to the conclusion that it would be much easier to kill him if 1) he was here at the office with me instead of home asleep in his bed; and 2) my brainwaves weren't reduced to brainripples since it is 3AM and the budget is due in six hours. I'll have to abandon the mental murder idea. On to Plan B: how to kill my boss using a partially consumed lukewarm Starbucks quad ten pump venti vanilla latte.

This isn't getting me anywhere. Murder probably isn't appropriate in a business situation and normally I wouldn't attack any of my coworkers with cold, milk-based drinks. How in the name of Thor did I end up like this? As best as my sleep-deprived memory can recall, it started with a phone call from my boss, Mr. Deadman. The phone rang; my heart sank.

"Sorry to bother you on such a lovely day," he said. I knew he was gazing at the sunset out his corner office window while I stared at my graying, windowless cubicle wall. At least I have that poster of a kitten clinging to a branch with the inspirational quote "Hang on... help is coming" to keep my morale up. I traded for it with the summer intern (he wanted the silver-plated pin with the company logo that I got for "5 years of dedicated service").

"No, no bother. Any questions on the consolidated budget? They're due tomorrow, so there *better* not be any questions. You know how I like to leave every day by 5." Since I hadn't left before 6 in this millennium, I laughed at my own semi-joke until I noticed that I was the only one laughing. He didn't say a word.

The silence stretched on like... something that stretches on for a really long time. As I stared at my kitten poster in hopes of salvation, he said, "Yeah...That's actually why I'm calling. I just need you to increase the IT hardware budget by 10%. Rising cost of servers, don't you know? No hurry, because I'm leaving for the day in just a couple of minutes. I won't even be able to look at the revised numbers until morning."

I could feel the anger rising as my morale sunk. I threw a pencil at the stupid kitten picture. Through gritted teeth, I managed to stammer, "Sure... no... problem..." and in my head I continued 'you jerk.'

With the perky voice of someone about to leave at 5:05PM, he said, "Excellent, and since it's no problem, can you do me a favor and analyze the IT budget growth since last year? I'd do it myself but I have a doctor's appointment first thing in the morning and I won't be in until right before the budget review meeting."

I imagined that I was the one hanging from that kitten's little tree branch. He took my momentary pause in entirely the wrong way. "Oh, don't worry, it's nothing serious. It's just a routine checkup but I figured I'd do it before year end when things are going to get really hectic. Well, have a great one. Don't work too hard, buddy."

He chuckled as he hung up the phone. Yes, he actually chuckled. I ripped the kitten poster off the wall and got back to work.

Updating the IT budget itself wasn't what took forever: it was consolidating all of our spreadsheets together. With over 200 Excel spreadsheets, I have to open up each one off the network share drive in exactly the right order, press F9, and then on to the next worksheet.

I ran into a frustrating situation around 11PM. After the initial submission of the budget sheets, someone had opened up his sheet and decided that his budget needed to be trimmed, so he deleted a column. My summary workbook, of course, wasn't smart enough to pick up on this change, so my formulas were adding in the wrong column. I noticed the issue around 11, but it took me until 3AM to find the source of the problem and correct it.

Now we're back to where our story began. Budgets have been consolidated, all errant formulas have been corrected, and I haven't even started on the analysis my boss requested. It's at this point that I realize that there's virtually no way to kill someone with a latte (even a really tasty and worth every dollar Starbucks latte) so I'd need to find a better plan. My eyes search my cubicle for implements of destruction.

My eyes wander past my red Swingline stapler and to my monitor where Excel is staring at me, mercilessly mocking me with its unnaturally straight gridlines. The numbers seem to be running across the screen and that's when I realize that I really need to take a nap. Wait. What is this menu item I see between Window and Help? Is this some salvation in the form of Essbase or is it just a mirage in the desert of my existence?

Choirs begin to sing as I realize that the key to my getting a few hours of sleep lies in the hands of a little Office add-in called Smart View and its good friend, Essbase. No, they aren't real choirs but rather my iPod playing Beethoven's Ninth, but surely this must be a sign.

Remembering everything I learned in that best-selling Essbase book I read, I raced to the Hyperion menu and within minutes had resubmitted my budgets, consolidated them, and performed some pretty amazing analysis. I finished everything just in time to sing along with Ode to Joy in gleeful gibberish German.

I must have fallen asleep, because the next thing I knew, my boss was standing at the entrance to my cubicle wearing golf attire. Doctor's appointment? Yeah, right. He spoke as I wiped the drool from the corner of my mouth.

"Wow, that outfit looks great on you. It looks even better on you today than it did yesterday. Say, what happened to your cat poster?"

It was balled up in my trash can at the moment, but I knew just where he should stuff it. I started to suggest it when he said, "I got the analysis you sent me at 4AM. I don't know how you got it done in time. It was wonderful."

Clearing thoughts from my head of relocating my poster into one of his orifices, I managed to eke out, "Thank you?"

He smiled and put his hand warmly on my shoulder. I didn't immediately try to break his wrist which meant that my thoughts of death by mind/coffee were gone only to be replaced (momentarily) with thoughts of a sexual harassment lawsuit.

"While I'd love to take the credit, Mr. Deadman, I have to say that I couldn't have done it without Essbase and Smart View. It saved my life last night" and yours too, I didn't add out loud.

He smiled from sunburned ear to sunburned ear. "Well, I always knew that buying Essbase was a good idea. I guess this proves it. You owe me one!"

He skipped off as I grabbed my copy of *Look Smarter Than You Are with Smart View and Essbase 11: An End User's Guide* and threw it at his head.

Note that the authors of this book do not condone in any way killing people with your thoughts, your latte, or your copy of this book. While the story above is fiction, similar situations occur all the time. We hope that you learn from this book so that you don't do something you might regret after enduring your 5-10 years of hard labor. Don't wait until 3AM to recall your Essbase teachings. Read this book, learn how to use Smart View and Essbase to your advantage, and please, get a good night's sleep.

Chapter 2:
The Beverage Company

A traditional computer book would begin at the beginning, giving you the complete history of the topic at hand from when the product was a twinkle in the eye of its creator through all the various versions up to the current, cutting edge product. This book will do no such thing. While we will cover the history of Essbase, let's first grab a beverage and actually learn to do something (connect to Essbase, retrieve data, learn about dimensions and members, analyze data, set options and more).

Imagine a company that sells soft drinks. The Beverage Company sells products across the United States and they want to find out which products and markets are profitable and which are losing money faster than their poorly named drink from 2001, "Diet Enron with Lemon."

To help with their analysis, they bought a product from Oracle called Essbase. They followed the more than 1,400 pages of instructions to get Essbase installed. During installation, they chose to install the sample applications and were pleasantly surprised to find that one of those applications was dedicated to analyzing The Beverage Company proving that Carson Daly and Earl were right about Karma.

To follow along as a temporary employee of TBC (**The Beverage Company**, *do* try to keep up), make sure that whoever installed Essbase at your company installed the sample applications. Until she's prepared the sample applications, you can either stop reading or follow along in your own mind instead of on the computer.

CONNECTING TO ESSBASE WITH SMART VIEW

Go ahead and launch Microsoft Excel. If you are in Excel 2007, you should see the *Hyperion* ribbon appear on your menu bar (in Excel 2003, you will find it under *Add-in* menu). At this point, temporary TBC employee, you're probably faced with a blank Excel workbook and you have no idea where to begin. Luckily, you have a book, so go up to the *Hyperion* menu and near the left side of the ribbon, you will see *Data Source Manager*:

Some of you will be saying "Wait, I don't see a ribbon. I'm on Office 2003." Never fear, you will find all of the same options under the Hyperion menu option. You'll use this menu for performing actions and should see all of the same commands like Zoom In and Refresh plus more. For those of you on Office 2007, you can also access the Hyperion menu for the full list of functions. This Hyperion menu is available under Add-ins ribbon:

Now where were we? Oh, yes, connecting to Essbase. Before you click *Data Source Manager*, though, notice some of the items in the *Hyperion* ribbon that we'll be using later. For instance, one menu option is *Refresh*. Presumably, we'll be using this to refresh data from Essbase. When we want to drill-down to detailed information, we'll be using *Zoom In*. When we need to send data back into Essbase (for budgeting, say), we'll use the *Submit Data* option. Before you begin to question whether or not you need this book if Essbase is going to be so darned easy to use, click *Data Source Manager*. From there click on the red text *Connect to Provider Services*:

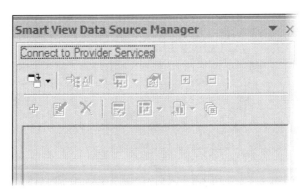

If this is the first time you've used the Smart View add-in, you may need to specify the URL to connect to the Hyperion Provider Services (don't worry, we'll come back to defining what in the heck the Provider Service is in a later section). You'll know this if the data source manager is empty or you are prompted.

Click the *Options* button on the far right section of the Hyperion ribbon:

Choose *Override Default* option and then type in the URL for the Hyperion Provider Services – something like http://*server*:13080/aps/SmartView (your administrator should be able to provide this to you):

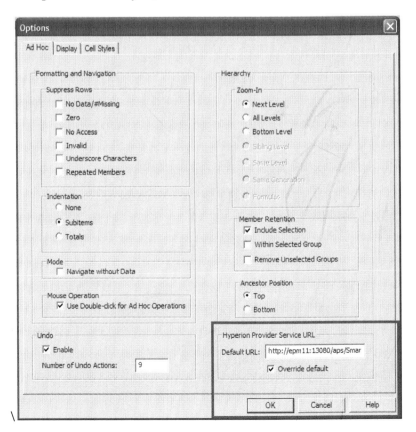

Click *OK*. Now you should see three folders: Oracle BI Server, Oracle Essbase, and Oracle Hyperion Planning. Click on the plus sign next to Oracle Essbase and you should see one or more Essbase servers.

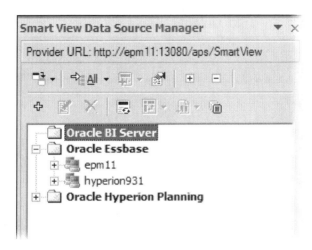

If you don't see the Essbase server, check and make sure you are viewing all connections:

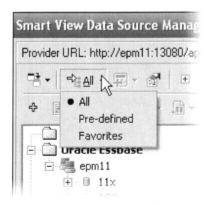

So what exactly is an Essbase server? Somewhere off in the basement of your company (or more likely these days, in a server farm in Malaysia) is a really powerful machine that holds the Essbase software and all of the data for the Essbase databases we'll be using. The sample applications mentioned earlier are stored on this server.

Your computer (which in computer terms is called the "client") talks to this server (through a networking protocol called TCP/IP, but you probably could care less about that). While all the data is stored on the server, all of the analysis happens on your client. Once we connect to the server, we can pull data back to the client and look at it in Excel. If we change the data, we should send it back to the server so that everyone else in the company can look at the same set of numbers. You've probably heard the saying "everyone is looking at a single version of the truth."

Before you continue, you need to know the name of your server as well as your Username and Password. Your login information controls access to various parts of the Essbase server. Depending on your Username, you might have access to the entire Essbase server, specific databases on the server, or you might have no access at all (in which case, this book will be somewhat unhelpful to you).

For instance, at my company, I am an Essbase administrator. In this God-like state, I am master of all Essbase databases. For the servers that I supervise, there is not a database that I cannot see, not a setting that I cannot change, and not a user that I cannot delete. While this does make me feel really special, it also means that whenever anything goes wrong, I am probably going to get blamed.

Only get Essbase access to what you need to do your regular job and avoid getting blamed for everything!
Tip!

The Username and Password given to you by your Essbase Administrator (see "God-like administrator" above) will grant you access to only some of the databases. Double click your Essbase server (again, if you're not sure which one is the right server, give your handy Essbase admin a call.)

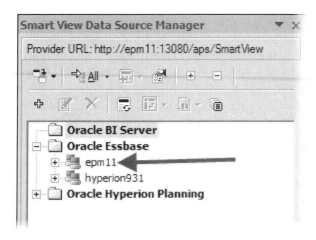

When prompted, enter your id and password. Click *Connect*:

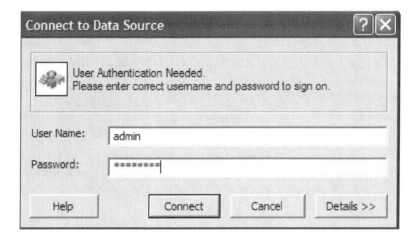

You will see a series of Applications appear in a list underneath the Essbase server (yellow cylinder icon denotes application). If you click the plus sign next to the application, you will see the databases (blue cube icon denotes Essbase databases or cubes).

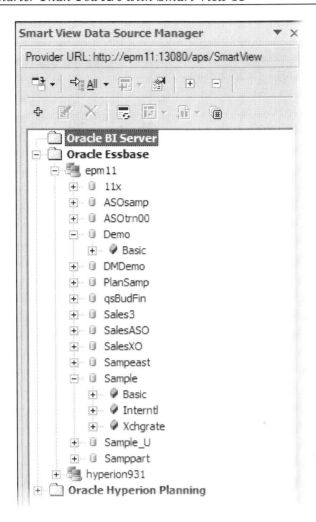

An Essbase application is a collection of one or more Essbase databases, but usually an application will contain only one database. In the image above, the Demo application has one database, Basic. The Sample application has three databases within it: Basic, Interntl, and Xchgrate.

Note!

If your company uses Hyperion Planning, the Essbase applications that support Planning often have more than one database and can have as many as five.

RETRIEVE ESSBASE DATA

The anticipation is overwhelming – you can't wait to start analyzing data. We'll be using the Basic database in the Sample application. We'll call it Sample.Basic, for short. Right click on the *Sample.Basic* database and choose *Adhoc Analysis*:

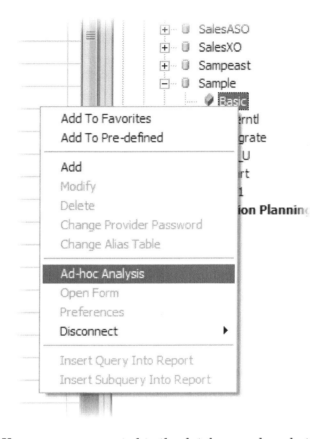

You are now connected to the database and ready to analyze data:

	A	B	C	D	E	F
1		Measures				
2	Year	105522		POV [Book1 ▼ ×		
3				Product ▼		
4				Market ▼		
5				Scenario ▼		
6				Refresh		
7						
8						
9						
10						

If you don't see the above grid, let's troubleshoot (and even if you do see the above grid, read along because at some point, you may see these issues). The first possible issue is that you might not see a number in cell B2. Instead of a number, there might be a dash or the word "#Missing" (more on that later). Or you also might see an error message:

Quite simply, the Sample.Basic database doesn't have any data. Nicely ask your Essbase Administrator to load the Sample.Basic database, right click on Sample.Basic and select *Adhoc Analysis* again, and you should see the spreadsheet grid shown above.

Before we start zooming and drilling (boy, Essbase sounds really exciting!), let's discuss connection information. The current spreadsheet tab in the current Excel workbook is the only one that's connected to Essbase. If you went from Sheet1 to Sheet2, Sheet2 wouldn't be connected. It is possible to click over to Sheet2 and connect it to Essbase, but at the moment, it's not.

This does bring up the interesting point that each sheet can be connected to a different Essbase database or no database at all. Sheet2 could be connected to Demo.Basic while Sheet1 is connected to Sample.Basic. All this can get a bit confusing and unfortunately in Smart View, there isn't a way to easily see the database you are connected to in the spreadsheet if you looking at all sources.

In the Data Source Manager, you can add your databases to *Favorites*. You can then change your view from *All Sources* to *Favorites*:

From there you can select and choose your data source in the *Activate* drop down selection in the Hyperion ribbon:

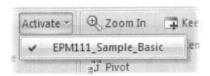

Now you know the database you are connected to within a selected spreadsheet. More on Favorites later in the book.

DIMENSIONALITY

Can we zoom now? Can we, can we? (My four year old just bounced into my head for a moment). Not yet. First let's define "dimensions", something you need to know before zooming and drilling can commence. Remember our initial spreadsheet:

	A	B	C	D	E	F
1		Measures				
2	Year	105522		POV [Book1 ▼ ×		
3				Product ▼		
4				Market ▼		
5				Scenario ▼		
6				Refresh		
7						
8						
9						
10						

What is a Dimension?

Those two words at the top of the spreadsheet (Year, Measures) and three words in the POV (Product, Market, and Scenario) are the dimensions of Sample.Basic. To oversimplify, a *dimension* is something that can be put into the rows or columns of your report (or it applies to the whole page). Different databases have different dimensions, and Sample.Basic has the five just mentioned.

Let go of your mouse for a second, and have a look at this really simple Profit & Loss Statement:

	Actual	**Budget**
Sales	400,855	373,080
COGS	179,336	158,940
Margin	221,519	214,140
Total Expenses	115,997	84,760
Profit	**105,522**	**129,380**

It only has two dimensions. Down the rows, we have our "Measures" dimension (often called "Accounts"). Across the columns, we have our "Scenario" dimension. Some people like to call this dimension Category, Ledger, or Version. It is Essbase tradition to call the dimension that contains Actual, Budget, Forecast, and the like "Scenario," and we'll follow the tradition.

The only two dimensions so far are Scenario and Measures. The more detailed breakdowns of Measures (Sales, COGS, Margin, et al) are the members of the Measures dimension. Actual and Budget are members in the Scenario dimension. A *member* identifies a particular element within a dimension.

If we pivot the Measures up to the columns and the Scenario dimension over to the rows, our report will now look like this:

	Sales	COGS	**Margin**	Total Expenses	**Profit**
Actual	400,855	179,336	221,519	115,997	105,522
Budget	373,080	158,940	214,140	84,760	129,380

While it doesn't look very good, it does illustrate a couple of important points. First, a dimension can be placed into the rows, columns, or the page (as we'll see in a second). If it's really a dimension (as Scenario and Measures both are), there are no restrictions on which dimensions can be down the side or across the top. Second, notice that the values in the second report are the same as the values in the first report. Actual Sales are 400,855 in both reports. Likewise, Budgeted Profit is 129,380 in both reports. This is not magic.

A dimension cannot be in both the rows and columns.

Note!

Three Dimensions

A spreadsheet is inherently two dimensional (as are most printed reports). They have rows and columns. This is great if your company only produces a Profit & Loss Statement one time, but most companies will tend to have profit (be it positive or negative) in every month. To represent this in Excel, we use the spreadsheet tabs (one for each month):

```
All Products and Markets.xls                      _ □ ×
                   Actual    Budget
      Sales        31,538    29,480
      COGS         14,160    12,630
    Margin         17,378    16,850
    Total Expenses  9,354     6,910
    Profit          8,024     9,940



  |◄ ◄ ► ►|  Jan / Feb / Mar / Apr / May / Jun / Jul / Aug / Sep / Oct / Nov / Dec /
```

We've now introduced a third dimension. Most people call it "Time" but Sample.Basic calls it "Year" just to be contrary. It could be across the columns (if you wanted to see a nice trend of twelve months of data) or down the rows, but we've put in the pages (a new tab for each "page"). That is, if you click on the "Jan" tab, the whole report will be for January.

If you're looking for Actual Sales of 400,855, you won't find it now because that was the value for the whole year. We could get it by totaling the values of all twelve tabs onto a summary tab.

Four Dimensions and More

Right now, this spreadsheet is not broken down by product or market. Within Excel, it's problematic to represent more than three dimensions (since we've used the rows, columns, and tabs). One way is to have a separate file for each combination of product and market:

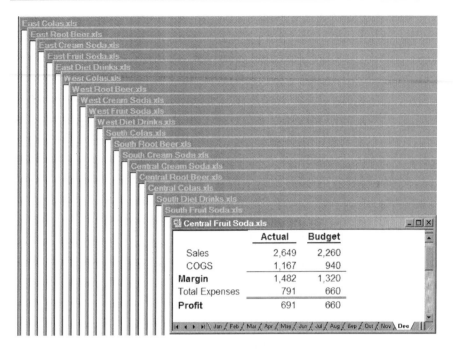

As you can see, this is getting ridiculous. What if we want to pivot our market dimension down to our columns so that we could compare profitability across different regions? To do this, we'd either have to have a series of linked spreadsheet formulas (which would break as soon as we added or deleted a new product or market) or we could hire a temporary employee to print out all the spreadsheets and type them in again with the markets now in the columns. While the latter method is obviously error-prone, the "rekeying" method is the one used by the majority of the companies in the world that do not own Essbase.

Since Market and Product are dimensions, it should be no more difficult to put them in the columns or rows than Scenario or Measures. As we'll learn about later, producing a report with markets down the side and products across the top is no more difficult than dragging-and-dropping:

		Actual	**Profit**	**Year**	
	Colas	Root Beer	Cream Soda	Fruit Soda	**Product**
East	12,656	2,534	2,627	6,344	**24,161**
West	3,549	9,727	10,731	5,854	**29,861**
South	4,773	6,115	2,350	–	**13,238**
Central	9,490	9,578	10,091	9,103	**38,262**
Market	**30,468**	**27,954**	**25,799**	**21,301**	**105,522**

In the bottom-right corner, you'll see our familiar actual profit for the year of 105,522. At the top of the report, you'll see that we have to specify the three dimensions in our application that are not in our rows or columns or Essbase wouldn't know which values to display. For instance, if we didn't specify "Profit", Essbase wouldn't know if we wanted Profit, Sales, Margin, or some random measure to be named later.

Tip!

Always specify a member from each dimension for each intersection. If Essbase doesn't know which member of a dimension to use for an intersection, it will use the topmost member of that dimension.

ANALYZING DATA

Now that we understand that a dimension is anything that can be placed in the rows, columns, or the page, let's get back to retrieving data and analyzing data.

Try It!

In case you weren't following along, go to a blank sheet in your workbook, connect to Essbase and then right click on Sample.Basic and select *Adhoc Analysis*.

Try It!

Go to another blank sheet in your workbook, connect to Essbase. Select Sample.Basic from the *Activate* drop down. Click *Refresh*.

You now have two spreadsheets that are connected to Essbase. Choose one and click on the cell that shows 105,522 and look at the formula bar just above the spreadsheet grid:

	A	B	C	D	
1		Measures			
2	Year	105522		POV [Book1 ▼ ×	
3				Product ▼	
4				Market ▼	
5				Scenario ▼	
6				Refresh	
7					
8					
9					

B2 ▼ f_x 105522

105,522 represents the total of all the months, products, and markets in our application, but notice that the content of the cell is not an Excel formula summing up other values. The total is being calculated on the Essbase server and then returned back to us as a plain, old number. This is one of the main reasons that Essbase is far faster than, say, a pivot table: all of the detail stays on the Essbase server and only the value we care about is returned to us.

Tip! Since there are no formulas linking this spreadsheet to Essbase (but only values), you can send this spreadsheet to people in your company who don't have access to the Essbase server.

Select the cell that contains *Measures* (cell B1 if you're following along). Measures tells us nothing, so go ahead and type the word "Profit" into that cell instead and press Enter. The numbers will not change, because you haven't told Essbase to re-retrieve your data yet. Choose *Refresh* from the ribbon:

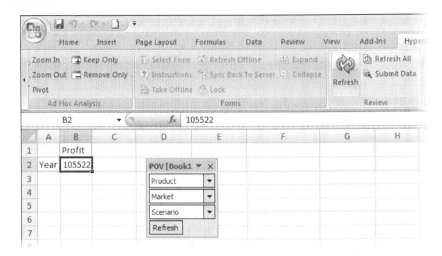

Now let's turn our attention to the POV. This floating window contains the other dimensions in the database that are not part of the spreadsheet. We can easily move these dimensions back and forth from the POV to the spreadsheet and back again. For example, select Scenario and drag it from the POV to the columns section of the spreadsheet, near Profit:

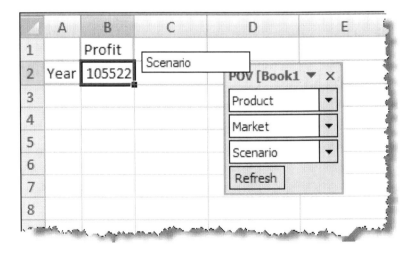

Scenario will be dropped into the grid either above or below profit depending on where you left your mouse:

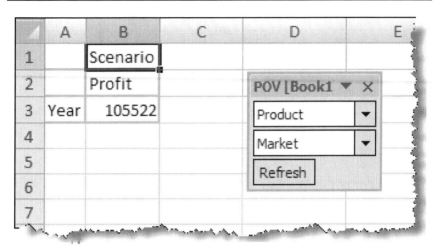

Next, let's update our analysis to focus on Budget. Type in "Budget" over Scenario and click *Refresh*:

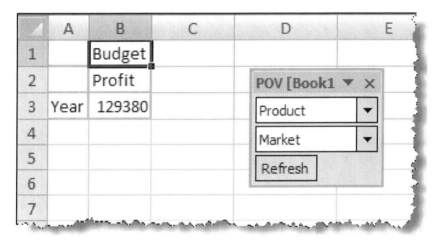

If you spelled Profit or Budget wrong, Essbase will kindly put the dimension it thinks you didn't specify into the POV for you. Type "Budgets" over "Budget" in cell B1. Click *Refresh*:

	A	B	C	D	E
1		Budgets			
2		Profit		POV [Book1 ▼ ×	
3	Year	105522		Product ▼	
4				Market ▼	
5				Scenario ▼	
6				Refresh	
7					
8					

Notice that cell B1 says "Budgets" so when we retrieved, Essbase put "Scenario" in the POV (thinking that we had forgotten a dimension). Essbase is very particular about spelling. It has no idea that "Budgets" and "Budget" means the same thing to you, so watch your spelling if you're going to be typing in the names of members.

Tip!   While spelling is important, members are not case-sensitive (unless the person setting up an Essbase application specified that it should be case-sensitive). Type in "BuDgEt" and Essbase will retrieve the data and replace your funky capitalization with "Budget".

Let's go through one more scenario: follow along with me. Open a new spreadsheet and type in the following:

	A	B	C
1		Actual	Budget
2	East		
3			
4			

Notice that we don't have a floating POV window and that we are not connected to a database. Right click *Sample.Basic* and select *Adhoc Analysis.* You should be prompted with the following message (maybe slight different but you'll get the gist of the message):

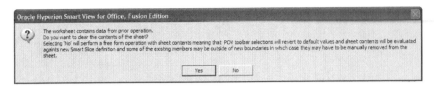

What Smart View is asking in easier terms: Do you want to remove the contents of your spreadsheet or do you want to keep them? The message also points out that if you are adhoc analyzing on a Smart Slice, certain things will happen (we'll cover smart slices later). We do not want to clear the contents of the sheet so we say no by clicking the *No* button. Now our spreadsheet is connected to the database and has retrieved values. The dimensions not specified in the spreadsheet were placed in the POV referencing the dimension member name.

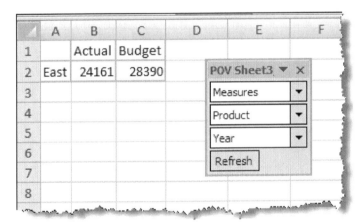

Go ahead and close this spreadsheet for now; we'll use the original query going forward. Are you ready to zoom?

Zooming In and Out

Assuming that your spreadsheet looks something like the following:

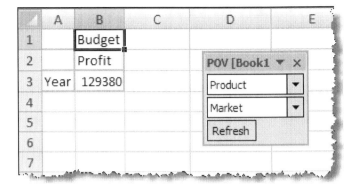

Select the cell that says Year (cell A3) and choose *Zoom In* from the Hyperion ribbon (you could also choose *Hyperion >> Adhoc Analysis >> Zoom in*):

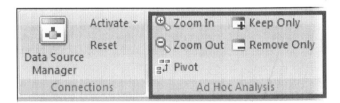

Though your report might not look exactly like this (depending on your current Essbase Options and Excel formatting), you should see the quarters that make up the total year:

	A	B	C	D
1		Budget		
2		Profit		POV [Book1 ▼ ×
3	Qtr1	30580		Product ▼
4	Qtr2	32870		Market ▼
5	Qtr3	33980		Refresh
6	Qtr4	31950		
7	Year	129380		

Select the Qtr1 cell (cell A3) and again choose *Zoom In*. This will show you the three months that comprise Qtr1.

Tip! There are also mouse shortcuts for zooming in and zooming out. To Zoom In using the mouse, double-click with the *left* mouse button on a member name. To Zoom Out, double-click with the *right* mouse button on a member name.

When we zoom in, we are navigating from the top of a dimension down the various levels, eventually getting to the bottom of the dimension. Zooming can also be known as drilling. In our example, we zoomed (or drilled) from Year to Quarter. Select Qtr1 and select *Zoom in* and we see the three months that make up quarter 1 – Jan, Feb, and Mar. We can zoom on any dimension in Essbase, quickly retrieving the data at various levels across the Essbase database (or for various member intersections within the database). For example, we've very quickly retrieved profit data for the three months that make up Qtr1 for all products and markets.

To go back up a dimension from bottom to top, you can either *Zoom Out*. Highlight any of those three months and choose *Zoom Out* from the *Hyperion* ribbon. Select a quarter and choose *Zoom Out* again and we're back to where we started.

If you are needing to "go back", Smart View provides Undo capabilities (that fortunately works great for undoing our actions in Smart View but unfortunately doesn't work anywhere else in our life).

Essbase Undo

To undo your last Essbase action, don't look under the *Edit* menu in Excel for Undo (and don't click the 🔄 button on the Excel toolbar). Simply click the *Undo* button on the Hyperion ribbon:

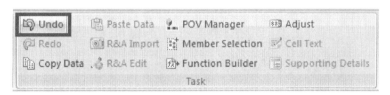

Note that you can also "Redo" which will reapply performed actions. How many times can you undo or redo? Well, it depends. Select the *Options* button from the Hyperion ribbon. On the Adhoc tab, you can define how many "undos" you would like Smart View to perform:

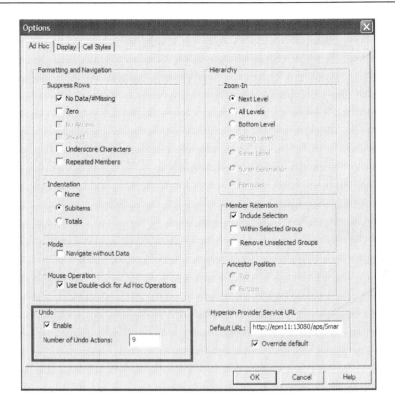

Tip!

If the Undo didn't work for you, make sure it is enabled under *Options >> Adhoc* tab.

You can type in the number of undo actions you want to allow. Should I set this number to 100? No, higher values can impact performance negatively so keep this number to just what you need.

Try It!

Assuming that your report is back to looking like the one above with only the quarters and the year showing, click on Qtr1 and choose *Zoom Out*. Either *Undo* or *Zoom In* to display the quarters again.

Keep Only / Remove Only

Let's say that you want to remove Year from the report. There are two ways to accomplish this. The first is by using the power of Excel: highlight row six and choose *Delete* from Excel's *Edit* menu. You can also use the power of Essbase by highlighting the Year cell and choosing *Remove Only* from the *Hyperion* menu. Try it – *Remove Only* the member Year. *Keep Only* is the opposite of *Remove Only*. It will keep the members you have selected in the spreadsheet.

Keep Only / Remove Only works on multiple cells as well. Select the Qtr1 cell, hold down the control key, and then click the Qtr2 cell. Now select *Keep Only*. Your report should be reduced to two quarters:

	A	B	C	D	E
1		Budget			
2		Profit		POV [Book1 ▼ ✕	
3	Qtr1	30580		Product ▼	
4	Qtr2	32870		Market ▼	
5				Refresh	
6					

Drilling, Dragging and Pivoting

Since this report is fairly useless, click on Qtr1 and choose *Zoom Out* to return to the previous report. *Zoom In* again to display the quarters above the year. Let's drill down a second dimension: highlight the Profit cell and choose *Zoom In*:

	A	B	C	D	E	F
1		Budget	Budget	Budget		
2		Margin	Total Expenses	Profit		
3	Qtr1	51540	20960	30580		
4	Qtr2	54780	21910	32870		
5	Qtr3	56410	22430	33980		
6	Qtr4	51410	19460	31950	POV [Book1 ▼ ✕	
7	Year	214140	84760	129380	Product ▼	
8					Market ▼	
9					Refresh	
10						

Now select Margin and click *Pivot* from the Hyperion menu:

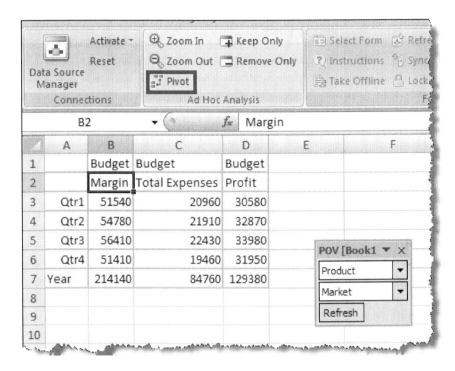

The result should look as follows:

	A	B	C	D	E	F
1			Budget			
2	Margin	Qtr1	51540			
3		Qtr2	54780			
4		Qtr3	56410			
5		Qtr4	51410			
6		Year	214140		POV [Book1 ▼ ×	
7	Total Expenses	Qtr1	20960		Product ▼	
8		Qtr2	21910		Market ▼	
9		Qtr3	22430		Refresh	
10		Qtr4	19460			
11		Year	84760			
12	Profit	Qtr1	30580			
13		Qtr2	32870			
14		Qtr3	33980			
15		Qtr4	31950			
16		Year	129380			
17						

Tip!

Did your retrieval look different, repeating the members Margin, Total Expenses and Profit for each time period? Select *Options >> Adhoc* tab and under the Suppression section, check Repeated Members. Click *Refresh* to update the spreadsheet.

We see how Smart View can show two dimensions on either the row or column axis at the same time. To get the quarters and years up to the columns, we could do that "hiring the temp to rekey method" we mentioned before, or we can do it the Essbase way. Highlight any of the member names in Year column, column B (Qtr1, say), and choose *Pivot*:

▲	A	B	C	D	E	F	G	H
1		Qtr1	Qtr2	Qtr3	Qtr4	Year		
2		Budget	Budget	Budget	Budget	Budget		
3	Margin	51540	54780	56410	51410	214140		
4	Total Expenses	20960	21910	22430	19460	84760		
5	Profit	30580	32870	33980	31950	129380		
6								
7							POV [Book1 ▼ ✕	
8							Product ▼	
9							Market ▼	
10							Refresh	
11								

Admit it: you're impressed. There is also a mouse shortcut for pivoting dimensions: it's called a "right drag-and-drop." Select the Qtr1 cell using your left mouse button. Now, with the mouse cursor over that cell, hold down the right mouse button. After a little while, a row of white member names should appear showing you what you're about to pivot. Don't let go of the right mouse button yet:

▲	A	B	C	D	E	F	G
1		Qtr1	Qtr2	Qtr3	Qtr4	Year	
2		Budget	Budget	Budget	Budget	Budget	
3	Margin	51540	54780	56 Year 5141		214140	
4	Total Expenses	20960	21910	22430	19460	84760	
5	Profit	30580	32870	33980	31950	129380	
6							
7							POV [Bo

Move the white cells over to the cell where you want to pivot the dimension. In our case, drag the members over to cell A3. Okay, now let go of the right mouse button:

▲	A	B	C	D	E	F
1			Budget			
2	Qtr1	Margin	51540			
3		Total Expenses	20960			
4		Profit	30580			
5	Qtr2	Margin	54780			
6		Total Expenses	21910			
7		Profit	32870			
8	Qtr3	Margin	56410			
9		Total Expenses	22430			
10		Profit	33980			
11	Qtr4	Margin	51410			
12		Total Expenses	19460			
13		Profit	31950			
14	Year	Margin	214140			
15		Total Expenses	84760			
16		Profit	129380			
17						

POV [Book1 ▼ ✕

Product ▼

Market ▼

Refresh

While you're back to having two dimensions on the rows, you've changed the orientation of the two dimensions to show each measure by each time period. If all we wanted to show for each time period was Profit, we can use the *Keep Only* function. Select one of the Profit cells (cell B4, say), and choose *Keep Only*. This will remove all the instances of Margin and Total Expenses (alternatively, we could also have used *Remove Only* on the other two members).

	A	B	C	D	E	F
1			Budget			
2	Qtr1	Profit	30580			
3	Qtr2	Profit	32870			
4	Qtr3	Profit	33980			
5	Qtr4	Profit	31950			
6	Year	Profit	129380	POV [Book1 ▼ ×		
7				Product ▼		
8				Market ▼		
9				Refresh		
10						
11						

This method is much more efficient than simply adding and deleting rows in Excel.

To clean up the report (since it looks a bit silly showing the same member repeatedly in the rows), again select one of the Profit cells and choose *Pivot*. Since there is only one member to be pivoted, Essbase will assume that you want the member to be pivoted up to the page instead of the columns.

Try It! At this point in time we're letting the reins go. Continue to play around with the features we've just illustrated. Try zooming in, zooming out, and pivoting the five dimensions of Sample.Basic. While you can make a very ugly report (no offense, but you *can*), you can't harm the data in any way: it's safely stored on the Essbase server.

Refresh the Data

You can refresh the data in a spreadsheet at any time. Let's say that you've stared at the same screen for three hours while you count down the number of seconds until your next vacation. Suddenly, your boss approaches and you're worried that she will see three hour old data and reward you with a permanent vacation. To refresh the data to the current values in Essbase, select the *Refresh* button:

You can also refresh the data by selecting *Hyperion* >> *Refresh* or *Refresh All*. Refresh All will refresh all worksheets in a workbook for the database connection. This is really helpful in instances when you've created a workbook of reports that you run on a regular basis. For example, you create and update your monthly reporting package each month. With one menu item, you can refresh the data for all reports within your workbook.

Aliases

Using your new Essbase knowledge, create the following query:

	A	B	C	D	E	F	G	H	I
1			Qtr1	Qtr2	Qtr3	Qtr4	Year		
2	Product	Margin	51540	54780	56410	51410	214140		
3		Total Expenses	20960	21910	22430	19460	84760		
4		Profit	30580	32870	33980	31950	129380		
5									
6							POV [Book1 ▼ ✕	
7							Market ▼	
8							Budget ▼	
9							Refresh	
10									

Zoom in on Product:

	A	B	C	D	E	F	G	H	I
1			Qtr1	Qtr2	Qtr3	Qtr4	Year		
2	100	Margin	15670	16890	17770	15540	65870		
3		Total Expenses	5880	6230	6330	5490	23930		
4		Profit	9790	10660	11440	10050	41940		
5	200	Margin	14920	15390	15580	15450	61340		
6		Total Expenses	6440	6550	6750	5650	25390		
7		Profit	8480	8840	8830	9800	35950		
8	300	Margin	11580	12620	12850	11650	48700		
9		Total Expenses	4610	4940	5140	4650	19340		
10		Profit	6970	7680	7710	7000	29360		
11	400	Margin	9370	9880	10210	8770	38230		
12		Total Expenses	4030	4190	4210	3670	16100		
13		Profit	5340	5690	6000	5100	22130		
14	Diet	Margin	14340	14910	15180	14250	58680		
15		Total Expenses	5430	5690	5800	5040	21960		
16		Profit	8910	9220	9380	9210	36720		
17	Product	Margin	51540	54780	56410	51410	214140		
18		Total Expenses	20960	21910	22430	19460	84760		
19		Profit	30580	32870	33980	31950	129380		
20									
21									

POV [Book1 ▼ ×
Market ▼
Budget ▼
Refresh

Note! Product does not equal the sum of the products underneath this, but it does equal the sum of products 100, 200, 300, and 400. Diet Drinks is a custom total that includes select products from the other product groupings. This is called an alternate hierarchy (discussed in detail in a later section).

Product 100 is doing very well this year especially compared to product 400. "100" is the member name of a specific Product member. Member names are the short "computer-like" way of referencing things that is completely unintuitive to the average user. Essbase allows member names to have longer, more user-friendly descriptions for members called "Aliases." For instance, the alias for "100" is "Cola". So how do we change the display from member names to aliases? First let's make sure the alias table is defined. You will use the Hyperion menu (not the ribbon). If you are on Office 2007, select *Add-ins >> Hyperion >> Adhoc Analysis >> Change Alias table:*

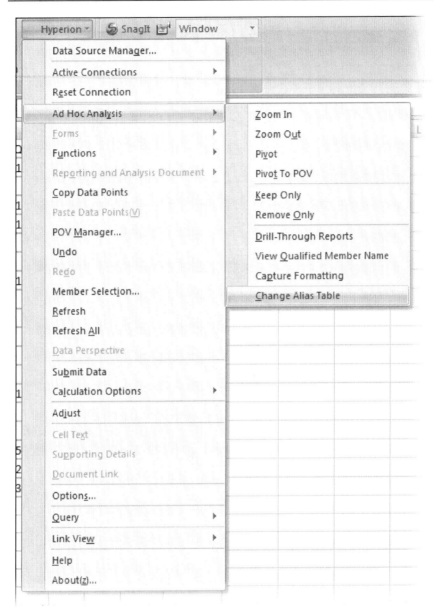

Note! Not all Essbase features and functions are available on the ribbon. You will have to use the Hyperion menu as well.

Select the *Default* alias table and click OK:

The spreadsheet will refresh with the aliases:

	A	B	C	D	E	F	G
1			Qtr1	Qtr2	Qtr3	Qtr4	Year
2	Colas	Margin	15670	16890	17770	15540	65870
3		Total Expenses	5880	6230	6330	5490	23930
4		Profit	9790	10660	11440	10050	41940
5	Root Beer	Margin	14920	15390	15580	15450	61340
6		Total Expenses	6440	6550	6750	5650	25390
7		Profit	8480	8840	8830	9800	35950
8	Cream Soda	Margin	11580	12620	12850	11650	48700
9		Total Expenses	4610	4940	5140	4650	19340
10		Profit	6970	7680	7710	7000	29360
11	Fruit Soda	Margin	9370	9880	10210	8770	38230
12		Total Expenses	4030	4190	4210	3670	16100
13		Profit	5340	5690	6000	5100	22130
14	Diet Drinks	Margin	14340	14910	15180	14250	58680
15		Total Expenses	5430	5690	5800	5040	21960
16		Profit	8910	9220	9380	9210	36720
17	Product	Margin	51540	54780	56410	51410	214140
18		Total Expenses	20960	21910	22430	19460	84760
19		Profit	30580	32870	33980	31950	129380
20							

If you type in a member, you can type in either the member name or the alias, and Essbase will be able to find it. For instance, below the cell with Product, type in the word "100-20" (without the quotes). "100-20" is the actual product member name. Re-retrieve your data and you'll see that Essbase replaced "100-20" with "Diet Cola". "Diet Cola" is the alias name.

Tip!

To type in a member name that Essbase could confuse with a number (like "100"), type in a single apostrophe before the member name. For "100", you would type in: '100. This tells Essbase (and Excel) that this is text and not a number.

Since some companies have multiple ways of referring to the same items (for instance, product 100 might be called "Cola" in the Northeast and "pop" in the Northwest), Essbase allows up to nine different aliases for each member. Right now, you're using the "Default" alias, but if your application has other descriptions for members beyond the defaults (called "alternate alias tables"), you can choose to use those in the drop-down box under Alias in the *Display* options.

Note!

Sample.Basic comes with another alias table called Long Names in addition to Default.

Note!

Select *Options >> Display* tab and note there is a section for displaying member names or descriptions. This is not available for Essbase connections. This section is used for Financial Management or Planning connections. A bit confusing, we agree.

OPTIONS

As mentioned before, your report might not look identical to the pictures in this book. The most common reason for this is that your Options have been changed. Options are tab-specific settings that control how Essbase operates. All of these settings are found by selecting the *Options* icon on the *Hyperion* ribbon.

Smart View options remembered as you perform analysis, across spreadsheets and database connections. They are not saved with individual spreadsheets or workbooks. For example if you turn on suppression of Repeated Members and you refresh data, any repeated members will be suppressed even if in the original spreadsheet you did not suppress. If you go to a new tab or new workbook (one that's never had the Options set) and retrieve, Smart View will use the Options that were last set.

Indentation

Notice that in our retrieves to this point, the detail beneath each member (for example, the quarters underneath the Year member) is indented. For those who went to accounting school prior to 1990, it might seem better to indent the totals. On the "Indentation" section on the Adhoc tab, you can switch the indentation from *Subitems* to *Totals*.

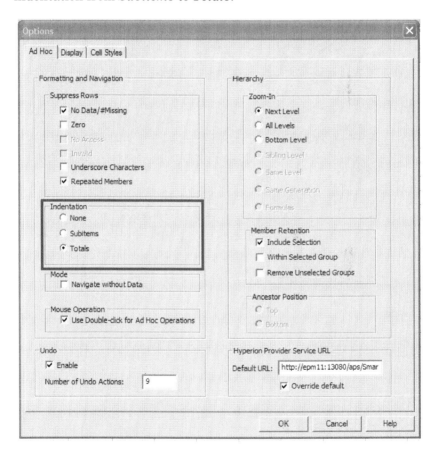

The next time you retrieve your data, each summary-level of totals will be further indented. See the example below where Quarters are indented from months and Year is further indented from the quarters:

	A	B	C	D	E	F	
1			Budget				
2	Margin	Jan	16850				
3		Feb	17330				
4		Mar	17360				
5		Qtr1	51540				
6		Qtr2	54780		POV [Book1 ▼ ×		
7		Qtr3	56410		Market	▼	
8		Qtr4	51410		Product	▼	
9		Year	214140		Refresh		
10	Total Expenses	Jan	6910				
11		Feb	6980				

To turn off indentation entirely, choose *None* under Indentation.

Zoom In Level

One of the other things that might have been changed under your options is the "Zoom In level." When you zoom in, you tend to want to see the members that comprise the current member. When you *Zoom In* on Year, you most likely want to see the quarters. Likewise, a *Zoom In* on Qtr1 should show the first three months of the year. Some impatient people don't like passing through the levels in the middle on the way to the bottom-level of a dimension. To control how far Essbase drills with each zoom, go to the Hierarchy section on the *Options >> Adhoc* tab:

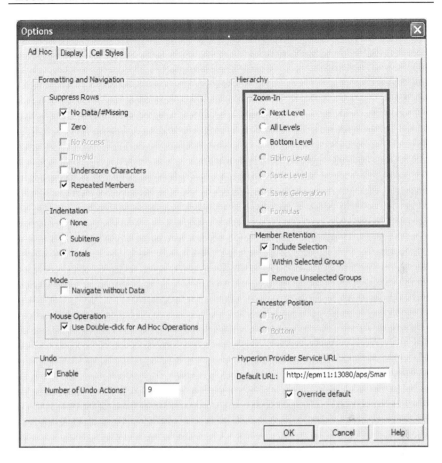

Right now, Zoom In is set to *Next Level*. This means that when you drill into Year, you see the quarters. If when you drill into Year, you want to see every single member in the Year dimension, set your Zoom In to *All Levels*. If you then drill on Year, you'd see every month and every quarter. If you want to jump from the Year down to showing all the months without showing any of the quarters, select *Bottom Level*.

Change your Zoom In level and then try zooming in and out on several dimensions. You can make a very large spreadsheet very quickly, and Essbase still remains
Try It!   extremely fast.

Before you drill into a dimension that has thousands of members, make sure that your Zoom level is not set to *All Levels* or *Bottom Level*. Sample.Basic has no dimension

Tip!   with more than 25 members, so you're safe for the moment.

The Member retention allows you to define what happens to the member that you drill on – do you want to keep it as part of the grid or remove it? If *Include Selection* is checked and you zoom in on Year, Year will still remain. If you uncheck this option, when you zoom in on Year, you will only see the children of Year.

Missing Data

On your *Options >> Adhoc* tab, review the available suppression alternatives: suppress no data/missing data, zeros, underscore characters and repeated members. Uncheck the box for *No Data / #Missing*.

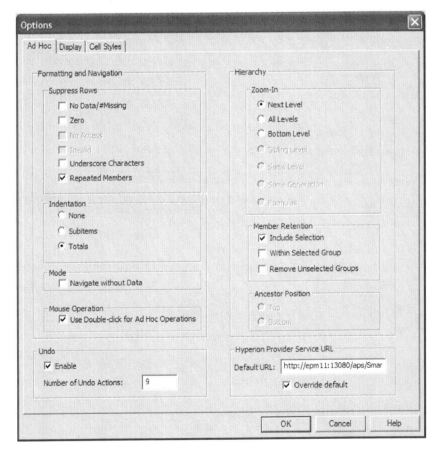

Select the Display tab and note the #Missing Label:

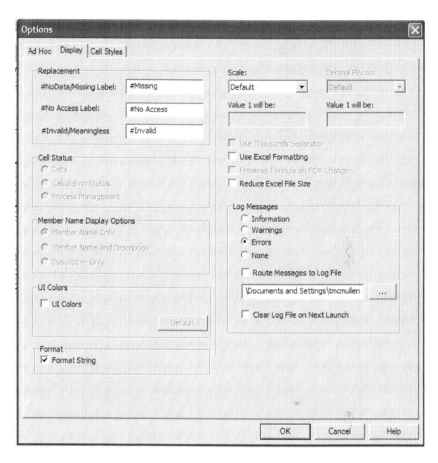

Click *OK* and go back to your report. *Keep Only* on Fruit Soda so that you only have data for the one product (one row). Now, drag Market into the report and click *Zoom In* on Market:

	A	B	C	D	E	F	G	H
1				Qtr1	Qtr2	Qtr3	Qtr4	Year
2	East	Fruit Soda	Margin	2450	2620	2740	2400	10210
3			Total Expenses	560	630	620	490	2300
4			Profit	1890	1990	2120	1910	7910
5	West	Fruit Soda	Margin	2910	3010	3130	2680	11730
6			Total Expenses	1490	1540	1550	1480	6060
7			Profit	1420	1470	1580	1200	5670
8	South	Fruit Soda	Margin	#Missing	#Missing	#Missing	#Missing	#Missing
9			Total Expenses	#Missing	#Missing	#Missing	#Missing	#Missing
10			Profit	#Missing	#Missing	#Missing	#Missing	#Missing
11	Central	Fruit Soda	Margin	4010	4250	4340	3690	16290
12			Total Expenses	1980	2020	2040	1700	7740
13			Profit	2030	2230	2300	1990	8550
14	Market	Fruit Soda	Margin	9370	9880	10210	8770	38230
15			Total Expenses	4030	4190	4210	3670	16100
16			Profit	5340	5690	6000	5100	22130
17								

Notice that the South is not a big fan of Fruit Soda. Budget Profit for the year is missing (denoted by Essbase with the term "#Missing"). A missing value to Essbase is very different from a value of zero. A profit of zero means that your sales were cancelled out exactly by your expenses. A profit of #Missing means that we have neither sales nor expenses at this particular combination. Data for Budgeted, South, Fruit Soda Profit for the year simply does not exist.

If you don't want to see #Missing on your reports, you can replace it with a label that makes more sense to you. Go to your Display options and in the box next to "#Missing Label", fill in something that makes sense to you:

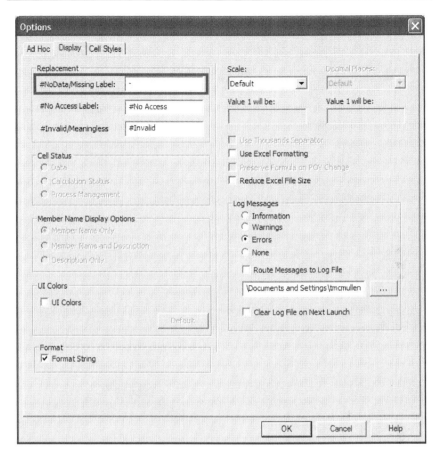

Tip!

The most common #Missing labels are: N/A, 0, -, and a space.

In general, there will be lots of intersections of data in your applications that don't exist, and retrieving them into a report takes unnecessary time. If you have 100,000 products and 5,000 stores, as few as 2,000 products might be sold each day at each store. Do you really want to see a report that's 98% empty? If you don't, check the box next to suppress *No Data / #Missing* on the Adhoc tab. This will suppress any rows where the data all the way across the row is #Missing. If a single column has a real number, the row will not be suppressed.

If you also don't want see intersections where all the values in the row are zero, check the box to suppress *Zero* as well.

Other Options

Navigate without data on the Adhoc tab allows you to set up your spreadsheet, defining the layout without the added time of retrieving data. This can speed up report creation time as you don't have to wait for Essbase to send the data. You can turn off mouse operations by unchecking *Use Double-click for Adhoc Operations*.

We'll cover a number of the other Essbase options throughout the rest of the book.

CHANGING DATA

Submitting Data

So far, all of your work with the add-in has been for reporting and analysis. One of the major uses of Essbase is for budgeting (or planning or forecasting or whatever you call putting information back into Essbase instead of just taking it out).

Using the techniques you've learned to this point, create a new report that looks like the following:

	A	B	C	D	E	F
1		Actual	Budget			
2	New York	678	640		POV [Book1 ▼ ✕	
3	Massachusetts	494	460		Sales ▼	
4	Florida	210	190		Cola ▼	
5	Connecticut	310	290		Jan ▼	
6	New Hampshire	120	110		Refresh	
7	East	1812	1690			
8						
9						

Tip!

To make a quick report, you can always type the member names into a blank spreadsheet. Put a zero where you want the numbers to appear, and refresh. Make sure that each intersection is represented by all dimensions.

The budget for cola sales in New York is looking a little light, so let's up it to 700. Type 700 into cell C2 (or wherever your report has the intersection of New York and Budget). Note the cell color changes to a yellow, highlighting an adjusted number. Choose *Submit*.

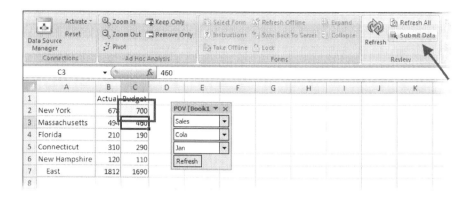

The data will automatically refresh showing you the saved 700 data value.

Now type in "Variance" next to Budget in cell D1. Click *Refresh:*

	A	B	C	D	E	F	G
1		Actual	Budget	Variance			
2	New York	678	700	-22			
3	Massachusetts	494	460	34			
4	Florida	210	190	20			
5	Connecticut	310	290	20			
6	New Hampshire	120	110	10			
7	East	1812	1690	122			
8							

This isn't going to make any sense but we want to show you a possible scenario that you could run into in your application. Type 50 in cell D2 (you're saying "what in the ..." but trust us). The cell shading will change to yellow. Now select *Submit:*

	A	B	C	D	E	F	G
1		Actual	Budget	Variance			
2	New York	678	700	50			
3	Massachusetts	494	460	34		POV [Book1 ▼ ×	
4	Florida	210	190	20		Sales ▼	
5	Connecticut	310	290	20		Cola ▼	
6	New Hampshire	120	110	10		Jan ▼	
7	East	1812	1690	122		Refresh	
8							
9							

Was the data saved to Essbase? Nope. Depending on the Essbase and security design, there will be some data points where you can't save data. In the case of Variance, this member is a dynamically calculated member and never stores any data. The other common causes are due to insufficient rights to edit those numbers and due to sending numbers into summary members (also called upper-level members).

Adjusting Data

One cool new feature we want to illustrate along with Submit is the Adjust feature. In Smart View, you can select a cell or cells and click the *Adjust* button. A window will display with some built in financial calculations to adjust the data set you've selected. Options include: Add a Fixed Value, Subtract a Fixed Value, Multiply Selected Cells by a Fixed Value, Divide Selected Cells by a Fixed Value, and Increase/Decrease Selected Cells by a Percentage:

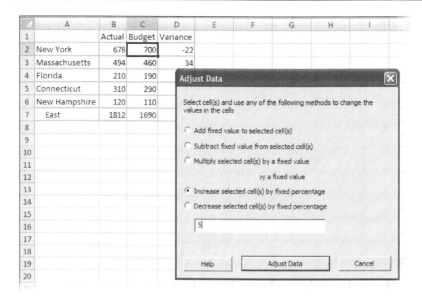

When you've adjusted the data, the data has not been submitted to the server. You have to click *Submit* to commit the changes back to the Essbase database.

When using Adjust, you must have Write security for the appropriate dimensions and intersections of data.

Note!

Adjust the budget for New York Cola for January by 5%.

Try It!

Running Calculations

If we were to submit 735 over the budgeted 700 value, math wizards in the audience will immediately note that 735+460+190+290+110 does not equal 1,690. It's actually 95 short, because we haven't told the Essbase server to recalculate the totals. For the most part, this is not done automatically. Many of the summary members in an Essbase application are "stored" meaning that Essbase stores the pre-calculated totals to speed retrieval. This follows the common Essbase belief that analysis tends to start at the top of the hierarchy and then drill down.

Note! One of the major differences between Essbase and a relational database is that relational databases assume that you want to look at detail (so displaying totals is much slower) and Essbase assumes that you want to look at summaries (though detailed data is not any slower).

Other members are "dynamically calculated" (though the cool kids say "dynamic calc") meaning that Essbase calculates those members at the time the user requests them. While some members in Sample.Basic are dynamically calculated (the upper-level Measures, for instance), it's always best to assume that you should recalculate the database after submitting data.

Assuming that you have access to recalculate the database, choose *Hyperion >> Calculation Options >> Calculate*:

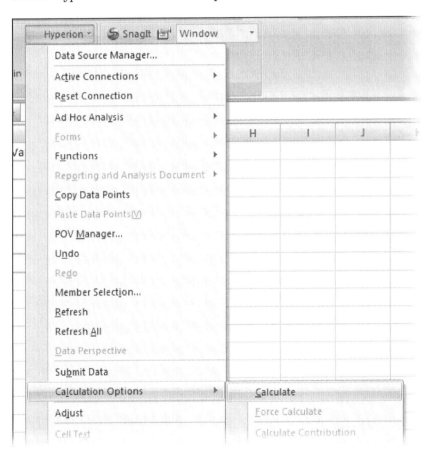

This will pull up a list of calc scripts for which you have access. You can filter this list by database. Select the calc script you wish to run and click *Launch*. In this example, choose Default for the Basic cube (basically means "calculate everything in the database that needs to be recalculated.")

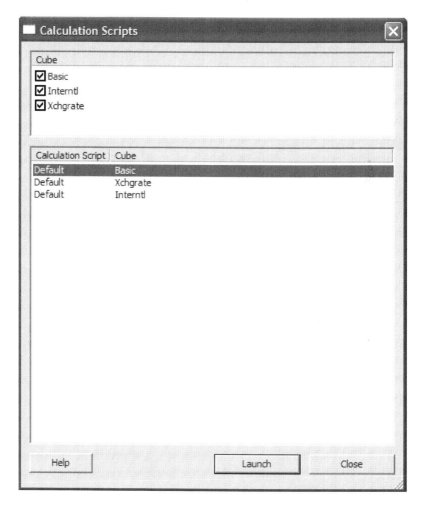

Smart View will check with the Essbase server every few seconds to see if the calculation has completed yet. You can always continue to work in Excel in the meantime, just don't work with this Essbase database unless you're okay with potentially erroneous results.

While the default calculation for Sample.Basic will always take just a few seconds, complex calculations against large databases can take several minutes or even hours. For instance, if your company had a multi-step allocation process that allocated corporate expenses by thousands of stores for thousands of products (to get a complete Income Statement by location by SKU), it would take a whole lot longer than five seconds. Be patient, and Smart View will let you know when the calculation is finished.

Once you get the calculation message, re-retrieve your data and you should see the correct value for East with the additional 95 in it:

	A	B	C	D	E	F	G
1		Actual	Budget	Variance			
2	New York	678	735	-57			
3	Massachusetts	494	460	34		POV [Book1 ▼ ✕	
4	Florida	210	190	20		Sales ▼	
5	Connecticut	310	290	20		Cola ▼	
6	New Hampshire	120	110	10		Jan ▼	
7	East	1812	1785	27		Refresh	
8							
9							

Logging Off

You can disconnect from a spreadsheet if you choose. Simply right click on the Essbase database and select *Disconnect*. You can also just close the spreadsheet and this will end your connection to the active Essbase database for the spreadsheet.

Can you believe it? You're already pretty sufficient in retrieving and analyzing data in Essbase. You successfully connected to an Essbase data, zoomed and pivoted, and set a number of options for analysis. Congratulations! But we're not done yet. Put down your mouse as we take a trip through history and also review some important fundamental concepts of Essbase.

Chapter 3:
What Does Essbase Stand For?

Essbase is currently produced by a company named Oracle. Prior to the earthshaking acquisition by Oracle, Essbase was produced by a company named Hyperion Solutions Corporation. Although Hyperion was founded in 1981, the Essbase product came along in the early 1990's compliments of a company whose only product was Essbase: Arbor Software. Up until 1998 when Hyperion and Arbor "merged", the two companies were fierce competitors who were just as likely to spit on each other in waiting rooms as work together. (We are kidding, but only slightly.)

Arbor Software was founded in 1991 by Jim Dorrian and Bob Earle. They noticed at the time that companies were beginning to use spreadsheets not just for presentation of information but as a place to store data and business logic. Often, multiple sources of data were being consolidated together in spreadsheets and they were even seeing companies begin to release analysis to the public based on data in spreadsheets.

Jim/Bob wanted to build a database for spreadsheets. Essbase actually stands for **S**pread **S**heet data<u>base</u> (the "e" was added to help folks pronounce the name correctly). Thanks to some creativity and some venture capital (of course) from Hummer Winblad, they released the first version of Essbase in 1992 (originally shown as eSSbase). This original release of the product garnered three whole paragraphs of press coverage in Software Magazine on May 15, 1992. Here it is in all its "babe in the woods waiting to be eaten by bears" naiveté:

DATA SERVER "FEEDS" 1-2-3 OR EXCEL

Arbor Software Corp.'s Essbase data server
Software Magazine; May 15, 1992

Following a three-year development effort, start-up Arbor Software Corp., Santa Clara, Calif., has built a data server that "feeds" popular desktop offerings, including 1-2-3 from Lotus Development Corp., and Excel from Microsoft Corp., on client machines.

"We conceded the front end to [widely installed] spreadsheets," said James Dorrian, president and co-founder. "We built the product with two assumptions: that people knew their spreadsheets and that people knew their jobs."

According to Marketing Vice President Michael Florio, the OS/2-based $22,000 Essbase offers users in client/server environments simultaneous access to large volumes of multidimensional spreadsheet data.

Notice that it was originally developed to run on OS/2 and its claim to fame was that it fed spreadsheets. Also, notice that you could get a copy for only $22,000 which sort of goes to show you that technology doesn't always get cheaper over time.

The first version of the product wasn't nearly as user friendly as it is today. Ignoring the Herculean steps required to actually build an Essbase database, retrieving data into Excel (or Lotus, at the time) required writing requests to Essbase in a language known as "Essbase Report Scripting."

	A
1	<PAGE (Measures, Product, Market)
2	Profit
3	Product
4	Market
5	<COLUMN (Scenario)
6	<CHILD Scenario
7	<ROW (Year)
8	<ICHILD Year
9	!
10	

But with time we came to know and love the Essbase Spreadsheet Add-in for Excel. When you chose *Essbase >> Retrieve*, you'd see a much friendlier interface:

	A	B	C	D	E
1		Profit	Product	Market	
2		Actual	Budget	Variance	Variance %
3	Qtr1	24703	30580	-5877	-19.21844343
4	Qtr2	27107	32870	-5763	-17.53270459
5	Qtr3	27912	33980	-6068	-17.85756327
6	Qtr4	25800	31950	-6150	-19.24882629
7	Year	105522	129380	-23858	-18.44025352
8					

The Essbase Add-in was everything we thought we needed for Essbase until Smart View came along.

INTRODUCTION TO SMART VIEW

What is Smart View? This may be a silly question because you used Smart View in the entire last chapter. But in case you missed it, Smart View is THE Office Add-in for all of the Oracle EPM System (formerly known as Hyperion) products including Essbase, Planning, Financial Management, Web Analysis, and Financial Reporting. It's Oracle's version of the Swiss army knife and that makes you MacGyver.

Many of you old Essbase users might think you're completely satisfied with the Essbase Spreadsheet Add-In for Excel (the old school add-in for analyzing Essbase data). Per Oracle, you are wrong. They do have a point: among other things, the Essbase Add-In only works in Excel. What if you want to pull some Essbase data into a Word document? What if you need to make PowerPoint presentations with tables that automatically update from Essbase? Well, your problems are solved by the Smart View Add-In.

When used in Excel, Smart View has similar functionality to the Essbase Add-In. Yes: two different tools to do the same thing. The navigation is a bit different in Smart View but you can drill down, swap rows and columns, etc. Why do we need two tools? Since there is a world-wide problem of starving computer programmers, one might speculate that Oracle is doing their part by keeping two development teams gainfully employed. But is there another reason?

Smart View takes Essbase reporting and analysis to another level above the Excel Add-in. With Smart View you can create reports in Word or PowerPoint with live data from Essbase sources.

Features like Report Designer, Query Designer, and Cascade (report bursting) give end users powerful reporting capabilities in the tools they know and love: Excel, Word and PowerPoint (beat that, Excel Add-in).

Smart View also brings Add-In functionality for all of the Oracle EPM products that need an Add-In. Smart View provides a single Excel interface for Financial Management and Planning, replacing the Planning Spreadsheet Add-In and HFM Spreadsheet Add-In. You can import Reporting and Analysis documents as images into Microsoft Word or PowerPoint. You can import query ready or fully formatted grids into Microsoft Excel. Is there anyone at this point that doesn't want to toss the Essbase Add-In on the 8-track tape trash heap of obsolescence?

This book focuses on how the Smart View Add-In works with Essbase, showing you how to perform ad hoc analysis in Excel and how to pull Essbase data into Word and PowerPoint. While we will not show you how to scramble an egg while it's still inside its shell, Smart View probably could do that too.

OLAP AND OTHER TERMS

When Essbase was first released, no one was quite sure what it was. Was it some sort of spreadsheet on steroids? Was it a temporary employee who was really good at typing? Was it a database? If so, why didn't it have records and fields and most importantly, why didn't it let IT geeks write SQL to access it?

Everyone was pretty sure what it wasn't: a typical relational database. The creators originally called it a "data server." Shortly after Essbase was created, they commissioned a study by the late Dr. E.F. Codd (the same Ph.D. who came up with the original rules for what constituted a true relational database) to determine what the heck Essbase was.

Dr. Codd was definitely impressed. He felt that this wasn't a relational database yet it was definitely a database and a very important new type to boot. He called it an "OLAP" database to separate it from every other database up to that point.

To put it simply, all databases prior to Essbase were built for the purpose of storing transactions. The goal for these systems was to get individual records into the database as quickly as possible and to get those same records back out again as quickly as possible. A side goal was to store that data in as small a space as possible, because those were the days when hard drive space cost as much as a good mule. Summarization of these types of databases was possible, but definitely not the objective of the database design.

Dr. Codd classified traditional relational databases "OLTP" (On-Line Transaction Processing).

He knew that Essbase was the first database designed purely to support analysis. Knowing that this was going to be The Next Big Thing, he created a term to describe these databases: OLAP (On-Line Analytical Processing). There were several features that Essbase offered that no previous database could handle.

Multi-Dimensional Databases

First of all, Essbase was a multi-dimensional database (MDDB or MDB, for short). What did the good doctor mean when he said Essbase was multi-dimensional? Simply that any of the dimensions set up in a database could be put in the rows or the columns (or applied to the whole page/report).

All databases up to this point were two-dimensional: records and fields. Essbase had no theoretical dimension limit (though there was certainly a practical limit). The Sample.Basic database we were accessing above has five base dimensions: Year, Measures, Product, Market, and Scenario. (It actually has five more "attribute" dimensions that we haven't even seen yet: Caffeinated, Ounces, Pkg Type, Population, and Intro Date.) The ASOSamp.Basic database is a sample Aggregate Storage database with 14 dimensions. The largest database we've ever seen had over 100 dimensions, but we think they were just trying to show off. In general, Essbase databases have five to ten base dimensions. By base dimension, we mean dimensions that show up all the time (like the five mentioned above in Sample.Basic).

While any relational database can be set up to give the appearance of having multiple dimensions, it takes a lot of up front work by developers. Essbase and other OLAP databases have dimensionality built-in.

Optimized for Retrieval

Essbase databases were also optimized for retrieval at any level of the hierarchy, even the very topmost number that might represent every dollar the company has ever made in its history. OLTP databases (relational databases) were nicely optimized for retrieval of detailed records but definitely not hierarchical information. By pre-saving summarized information, Essbase allows analysis to happen from the top down with no decrease in performance.

For OLAP databases, the hierarchy is native to the database itself. This is far different from relational databases that store the data in one table and then have one or more other tables that can be joined in to view data in a rolled-up fashion. For Essbase, the hierarchy is the database. When you change the hierarchy logic in Essbase as to how a product is grouped or a market rolls-up, you actually change where the data is stored.

Because hierarchy is inherent to OLAP databases, drill-down (sometimes known as "slicing and dicing" but never known as "making julienne data") is inherent as well. Essbase is great at doing Ad hoc analysis (see Chapter 2) because it knows that when a user double-clicks on Qtr1, she wants to see Jan, Feb, and Mar. This is because the roll-up of months to quarters is pre-defined back on the server.

Dr. Codd came up with ten rules for defining OLAP databases. Some of them (such as the ability to write-back data) were more interesting than others. While some other databases at the time met one or more of the qualifications, the only OLAP database to meet all ten was Arbor Software's Essbase. (Remember that Arbor is the company that commissioned the study.)

DSS, EIS, BI, BPM, EPM...

For the first few years, everyone called Essbase (and its competitors like Cognos and Business Objects) either an MDDB or OLAP database. The problem was that this was very difficult to explain to a casual user. Since casual users (CEOs, COOs, CFOs, etc.) are the ones who tend to sign checks at most companies, this produced a marketing problem of the highest order. What is the actual purpose of these OLAP databases?

The overarching belief was that OLAP/MDDB databases "helped users make decisions and then provide them the information they needed to support those decisions." Since HUMDATPTTITNTSTD makes for a lousy acronym, the term DSS was created and thus the "Decision Support Systems" term was coined.

Since 1992 when Essbase was released, other terms have been bandied about at various times including EIS (either "Executive Information Systems" or "Enterprise Information Systems" depending on whom you ask) and BI (Business Intelligence). Business Intelligence is still used fairly frequently (thanks to a well funded marketing campaign by IBM in the late 90's), but its popularity is quickly being overtaken by BPM.

BPM (Business Performance Management) and more recently EPM (Enterprise Performance Management) is meant to include BI and expand it to also include any information a user needs to manage the performance of her company. Nowadays, this goes well beyond just a database and includes applications such as scorecarding, planning, and financial consolidation. If there is a number that needs to be manipulated, rolled-up, sliced, or diced, BPM should be able to handle it whether the original number is in an OLAP or OLTP database.

Historically, Essbase (and pretty much every other product Hyperion made) has been seen as a financial tool. The reason for this is two-fold. First, financial minds tend to understand Essbase really well. Financial analysis is inherently multi-dimensional. Income Statements tend to have accounts, time periods, scenarios, organizations, departments, companies and years on them. Since relational databases do a poor job at multi-dimensional data, finance types started using spreadsheets. Since Essbase was a database for spreadsheets, it made it really easy to explain the value to CFOs, Controllers, VPs of Planning, and the like.

The second reason for Essbase's traditional stereotyping as "something the bean counters use" has to do with sales and marketing. Since Essbase was so easy to explain to end users in accounting and finance, that's the group that the Essbase sales representatives tended to call on. The sad part about this is that the IT organization often felt left out and turned to inferior products from competing vendors because those vendors were seen as developing products that were more "IT-centric."

As for the current market, Oracle is generally accepted to be the market leader in the EPM space. They should be since they created the term in the first place in the early 21st century. EPM is quite the hot software niche these days thanks in no small part to Sarbanes-Oxley bringing compliance and management of data to the forefront. Simply put, Sarbanes-Oxley can put you in jail, and EPM can help keep you out.

Tip!

Putting Essbase, Hyperion, and EPM on your resume may very well get you a 10% boost in salary at your next job. Feel free to share half of that with the authors of this book.

ESSBASE TERMINOLOGY

We managed to make it all the way through the last chapter without learning a lot of Essbase terminology, but to truly succeed in the world of Essbase, there are some handy terms to pick up. Some of them we've already learned.

A "dimension" defines different categories for your data. A dimension can be located on the rows, columns, or pages of your queries. A "member name" is the short, computery name for the member of an Essbase dimension (like "100-10"). An "alias" is the longer, more descriptive name for a member (like "Cola"). All of the dimensions in a database make up the "outline."

Here is a portion of Sample.Basic outline:

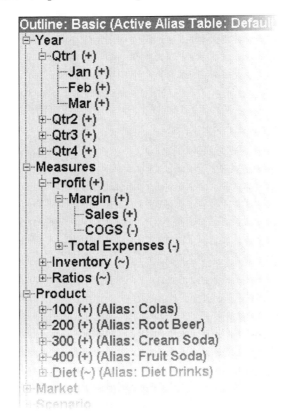

Family Tree Relationships

The most common way to refer to members in an outline relative to each other is by using "family tree" relationships. The members directly below a member are called its children. For instance, the Product dimension has five children: Colas, Root Beer, Cream Soda, Fruit Soda, and Diet Drinks. If we ever wanted to refer to those members on a report without hard coding them, we could say "give us all the children of Product."

The advantage to this aside from the saving in typing is that if a new product line was to be added (say, "Water"), we wouldn't have to modify our reports. Any report designed to display the children of Product would pick up the new "Water" product and add it to the list automatically.

If Colas, Root Beer, and the other rug rats are all the children of Product, what relation is Product to its children? Assuming you didn't fail "Birds and the Bees 101," you'll know that Product must be the *parent* of Colas, Root Beer, and the rest. In other words, the parent of any member is the one that the member rolls-up into. Qtr2 is the parent of May. Year is the parent of Qtr2.

Since Colas and Root Beer are both the children of Product, Colas and Root Beer are siblings. This is simple, but what relationship do January and May have? Well, their parents are siblings so that makes them... cousins. Correct, but "cousins" while technically correct isn't used that often. In general, people say that January and May are at the "same level."

What if you want to refer to all the members into which May rolls (not just the one right above)? Well, those are its ancestors which in this case would be Qtr2 and Year. Correspondingly, the descendants of Year would include all four quarters and all twelve months.

Note that there are members that don't have any children. In the picture above, May is childless. We refer to childless members as being "level-0". If you ever want all of the bottom, childless members of a dimension, just ask for the level-0 members. For example, the level-0 members of the Year dimension are the months and the level-0 members of the Market dimension are the states.

Level-0 members are sometimes also referred to as "leaves," because they're at the edges of the family tree. Edward sometimes refers to level-0 members as "the ones who aren't allowed to sit at the main table on Thanksgiving," but we think he is the only one.

All of the parents of the level-0 members are referred to as level-1. Since the level-0 members of the Year dimension are the months, then the level-1 members are the quarters. For the Market dimension, the level-1 members are the regions: East, West, South, and Central.

Just as the parents of the level-0 members are level-1 members, the parents of level-1 members are level-2 members. Their parents are level-3 members and so on up the hierarchy. There are many places in Essbase that you can specify, for example, "All the level-2 members of the Product dimension," so remember that levels count up from the bottom of a dimension starting at 0.

If you want to count down the hierarchy, use generations instead of levels. The dimension itself is considered generation-1 (or "gen1," for short). Its children are gen2. For the Year dimension, the gen2 members are the quarters.

Yes, the quarters are both level-2 and generation-2. Why do we need both levels and generations? Well, in some dimensions with many, many levels in the hierarchy, you'll want to count up from the bottom or down from the top depending on which you're closer to. We've seen a dimension with 17 levels in the hierarchy, and it definitely was nice to have both options available to me. The children of gen2 members are gen3 and so on down the hierarchy.

Why do generations start counting from 1 and levels from 0? It's because generation 0 is considered to be the outline itself making its children, the dimensions, generation 1.

Note!

While counting with generations is pretty straight-forward, levels can sometimes be a bit tricky. Look at this portion of the Measures dimension from Sample.Basic:

For this dimension, Gen1 is Measures. Gen2 is Profit and Inventory. Gen3 is Margin, Total Expenses, Opening Inventory, Additions, and Ending Inventory.

So far this is looking pretty easy, but let's switch our focus to the levels. The level-0 members are Sales, COGS, Marketing, Payroll, Misc, Opening Inventory, Additions, and Ending Inventory. The level-1 members are Margin, Total Expenses, and Inventory. What are the level-2 members? Profit (because it's the parent of level-1 members Margin and Total Expenses) and Measures (because it's the parent of level-1 member Inventory).

The trickiness is that Measures is *also* a level-3 member because it's the parent of Profit, a level-2 member. This means that if you ask Essbase for level-2 members, you'll get Measures, but you'll also get Measures if you ask for level-3 members. Notice that this counting oddity does not occur with generations.

Note!

This instance of a dimension is also known as a ragged hierarchy.

Time to pick up your mouse and get moving again. Let's work those Essbase muscles and learn the skills we need like member selection and data points to become a power Essbase user.

Chapter 4:
Become a Power User

Up to this point, we've primarily been navigating our way to data by either zooming in or out, using keep/remove only, or just typing members into our spreadsheet. In this chapter, we'll introduce you to member selection capabilities, the Smart View Query Designer, the POV Manager and more: all tools that will help you get the information you need faster and easier.

What if your boss, let's call him Lumbergh, requested a detailed market report analyzing financials by state just as you were about to duck out for the weekend. Despite your attempts to avoid him at the end of the day on Friday (one can only hide in the copy room for so long), he catches you with an "I'm gonna need you to go ahead and come into tomorrow" to get the state analysis done.

You could create this sheet by opening up a blank spreadsheet, typing Measures into cell B1, Product into C1, Scenario into D1, all the months into B2:B13, and all the states into the cells starting at A3.

	A	B	C	D	E	F	G	H	I	J	K	L	M	N	O	P
1		Jan	Feb	Mar	Apr	May	Jun	Jul	Aug	Sep	Oct	Nov	Dec			
2	New York	512	601	543	731	720	912	857	570	516	766	721	753			
3	Massachusetts	519	498	515	534	548	668	688	685	563	477	499	518			
4	Florida	336	361	373	408	440	491	545	529	421	373	337	415			
5	Connecticut	321	309	290	272	253	212	198	175	231	260	310	262			
6	New Hampshire	44	74	84	86	99	125	139	136	93	81	75	89			
7	California	1034	1047	1048	1010	1093	1185	1202	1269	1122	1053	923	978			
8	Oregon	444	417	416	416	400	402	414	412	409	421	467	444			
9	Washington	405	412	395	368	378	372	372	392	394	397	385	371			
10	Utah	237	251	256	277	262	246	276	248	217	269	309	307			
11	Nevada	219	267	289	330	365	411	493	451	268	317	281	348			
12	Texas	504	547	531	507	547	556	556	595	552	531	497	502			
13	Oklahoma	241	234	243	277	279	306	335	338	292	284	309	353			
14	Louisiana	259	263	251	228	231	227	202	253	262	302	279	235			
15	New Mexico	-7	2	9	28	38	43	78	48	4	13	23	51			
16	Illinois	912	963	980	1036	1102	1160	1237	1191	1025	1017	915	1039			
17	Ohio	384	362	357	370	359	363	378	347	352	330	395	387			
18	Wisconsin	297	307	309	287	303	310	315	334	307	284	247	247			
19	Missouri	125	132	142	151	133	104	135	80	79	101	139	145			
20	Iowa	653	677	706	734	781	821	854	871	786	739	662	777			
21	Colorado	585	622	596	594	598	620	604	621	596	638	594	559			
22	New York	512	601	543	731	720	912	857	570	516	766	721	753			
23	Massachusetts	519	498	515	534	548	668	688	685	563	477	499	518			
24	Florida	336	361	373	408	440	491	545	529	421	373	337	415			
25	Connecticut	321	309	290	272	253	212	198	175	231	260	310	262			
26	New Hampshire	44	74	84	86	99	125	139	136	93	81	75	89			
27	California	1034	1047	1048	1010	1093	1185	1202	1269	1122	1053	923	978			
28	Oregon	444	417	416	416	400	402	414	412	409	421	467	444			

POV Sheet3 ▼ ✕
Measures ▼
Product ▼
Scenario ▼
Refresh

This, however, would mean coming in on Saturday. Is there another way to get this done and save your plans for organizing the sock drawer? Alternatively, you can use a previously ignored menu item called *Member Selection.*

MEMBER SELECTION

Member Selection Basics

Member Selection is like your own personalized temp typist. Let's see how handy he can be at generating spreadsheets like the one above. First, we'll make Member Selection (often shortened to Member Select) type in our states for us.

In a blank worksheet, right click on *Sample.*Basic and select *Adhoc Analysis.* Drag the Market dimension to rows and the Year dimension to the column. Move Measures back to the POV. You spreadsheet should look something like this:

On your default query, select cell A2 and then choose the *Member Selection* button:

The Member Selection window will display:

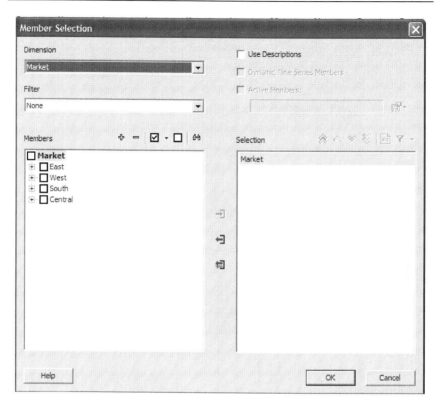

Notice that the dimension that comes up is Market. Smart View will retrieve dimension you want to use for picking members based on what's in the cell you currently have selected. Select a blank cell and try clicking *Member Selection*. What do you see?

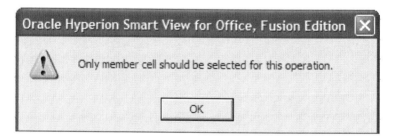

You could also see a Dimension Name Resolution screen which allows you to pick the desired dimension and the desired orientation for the spreadsheet (e.g. vertical position to list members down the page). As you can see, layout is very important when defining queries and using member selection.

Back to the task at hand, let us take a closer look at the Member Selection window:

The members in the left box should change to show the Market dimension. Click the plus sign next to East and it will expand to show you the states in the East. Click the check box for the all of the East states:

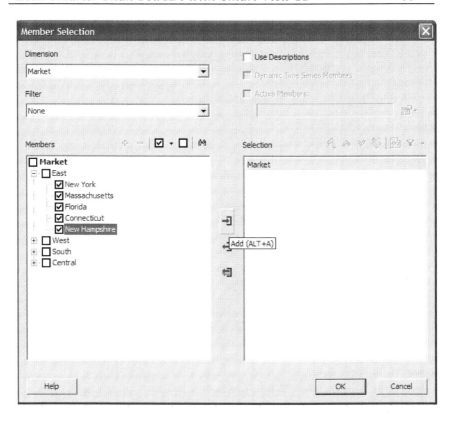

Now click the -> *arrow* button. You should now see five of the fifty most important states in the USA appear in the box to the right under Selection. Use this same method to add the states under West, South, and Central to the list on the right. You should now be looking at the following:

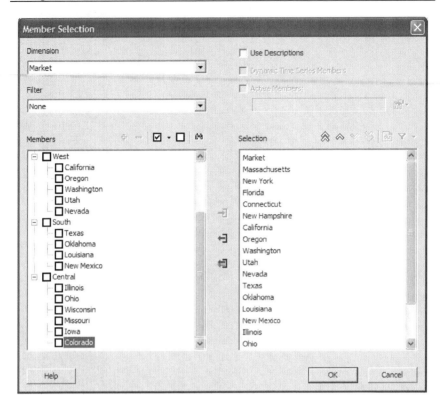

If you're an obsessive-compulsive type and want to manually alphabetize your state names before entering them into the sheet, highlight the state you want to rearrange in the list and then click either the *Move Item Up* or *Move Item Down* buttons:

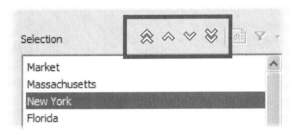

If you accidentally add any member more than once, highlight the member to remove and choose the <- *arrow* icon. To clear the whole list, click the double arrow icon:

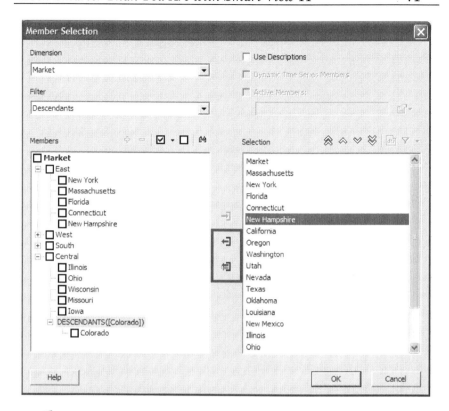

 Note!

Try to shift+click or control+click to select multiple members. Unfortunately it doesn't work but don't worry, we'll show you more tips for selecting members.

Assuming your list is complete (and alphabetized if that's how you roll), click *OK* and you'll be able to watch while Essbase enters the states down the left side of your spreadsheet.

 Note!

After you use Member Selection to type in your members, you will need to choose *Refresh* yourself. Member Selection does not do a retrieve on its own.

Let's use a slightly different method to type in the months. Select cell B1 and choose *Member Selection*. The Year dimension should appear. Under "Filter", choose *Level*:

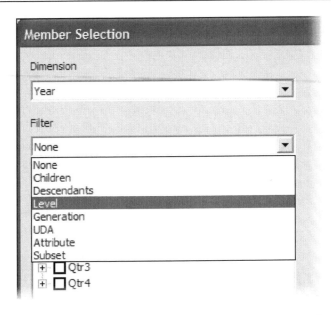

Remember that the months are level-0 since they don't have any children (through no lack of trying, mind you). Enter the level number in this case, 0:

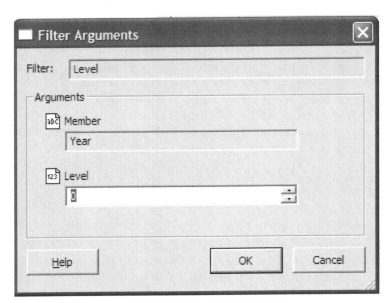

 You could also use the arrow keys to select the available levels for the selected dimension.

Tip!

Click *OK* and you will see the level zero months are available in the Members section. Note they haven't been selected yet. We've only filtered them in the Members section:

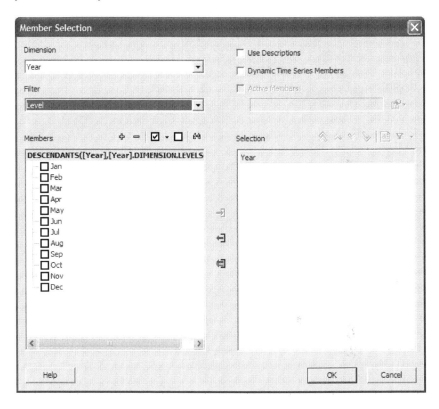

Click the *Check mark* icon (between the minus and blank square icons) to select all of the months (much easier than having to manually check month by month):

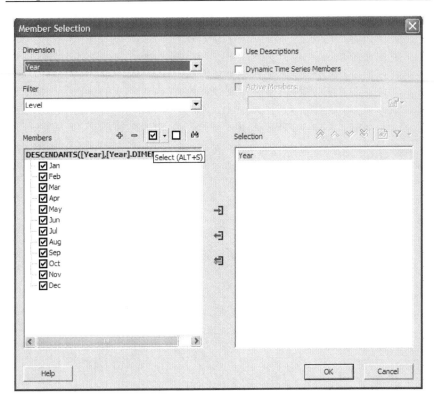

Now move the months over to the Selection section by clicking the right arrow icon . Click *OK* and the months are placed across the columns in your spreadsheet:

Smart View intuitively knows to place the months across the columns whereas in the old Excel Add-in, you had to **Note!** manually check a box to place selections across the columns.

Remember to refresh to see the data.

More Member Selection Options

What about changing the members that are displayed in my POV? We'll follow a similar process but before we get there, let's do one thing. Go to *Hyperion>> Adhoc Analysis >> Change Alias Table* and select Default. Remember, this is the way you toggle back and forth between member names and aliases in Smart View.

Tip!

You have to set the alias table for each new connection to a spreadsheet. The default alias table for a connection is *None*.

Select the drop down arrow next to Product and choose the ellipses (…).

The Member Selection window is launched:

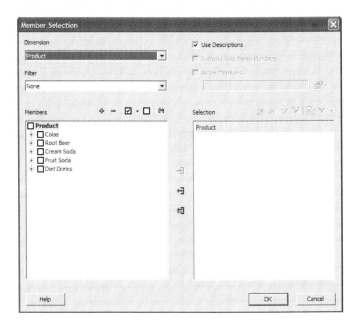

Notice the *Use Descriptions* check box is checked now that we have chosen an alias. Uncheck this box. Nothing changes, right? This check box is only applicable for FM and Planning sources.

Let's say we want to perform analysis on the Diet Drinks. Check the Diet Drinks check box and then select children under the Select icon:

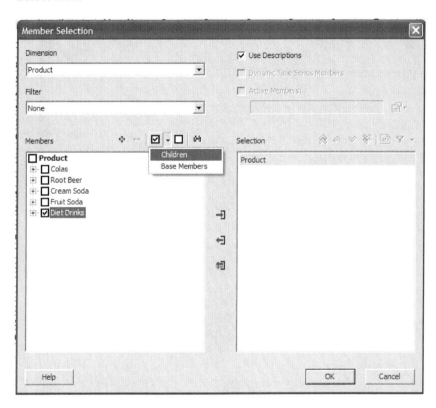

The children of Diet Drinks are automatically expanded and selected. If we had chosen Base Members, the level zero members would have been displayed and selected (in this case the same as children). Move the Diet Drinks members over to the Selection section and click *OK*.

Now in the Product drop down, all selected members are available:

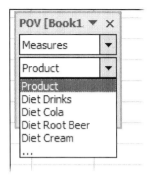

Change the selection from Product to Diet Drinks and click *Refresh* to see the new data.

Drag the Product dimension into the rows on the other side of Market. WOW! That was a really fast way to view diet drink performance across markets (Lumbergh is going to be really excited about this level of detail and it is only 5:15 on Friday; no Saturday work for you):

	A	B	C	D	E	F	G	H	I	J	K	L
1			Jan	Feb	Mar	Apr	May	Jun	Jul	Aug	Sep	Oct
2	Product	Market	8024	8346	8333	8644	8929	9534	9878	9545	8489	8653
3		Massachusetts	519	498	515	534	548	668	688	685	563	477
4		New York	512	601	543	731	720	912	857	570	516	766
5		Florida	336	361	373	408	440	491	545	529	421	373
6		Connecticut	321	309	290	272	253	212	19		231	260
7		New Hampshire	44	74	84	86	99	125	13		93	81
8		California	1034	1047	1048	1010	1093	1185	120		122	1053
9		Oregon	444	417	416	416	400	402	41		409	421
10		Washington	405	412	395	368	378	372	372	392	394	397
11		Utah	237	251	256	277	262	246	276	248	217	269
12		Nevada	219	267	289	330	365	411	493	451	268	317
13		Texas	504	547	531	507	547	556	556	595	552	531
14		Oklahoma	241	234	243	277	279	306	335	338	292	284
15		Louisiana	259	263	251	228	231	227	202	253	262	302
16		New Mexico	-7	2	9	28	38	43	78	48	4	13
17		Illinois	912	963	980	1036	1102	1160	1237	1191	1025	1017
18		Ohio	384	362	357	370	359	363	378	347	352	330
19		Wisconsin	297	307	309	287	303	310	315	334	307	284
20		Missouri	125	132	142	151	133	104	135	80	79	101
21		Iowa	653	677	706	734	781	821	854	871	786	739
22		Colorado	585	622	596	594	598	620	604	621	596	638
23	Diet Drinks	Market	2279	2362	2376	2396	2434	2506	2610	2595	2327	2379
24		Massachusetts	#Missing	#Missing	#Missing	#Missing	#Missing	#Missing	#Missing	#Missing	#Missing	#Missing
25		New York	#Missing	#Missing	#Missing	#Missing	#Missing	#Missing	#Missing	#Missing	#Missing	#Missing
26		Florida	151	156	163	187	197	203	236	193	160	146
27		Connecticut	30	29	26	24	22	19	16	16	23	21
28		New Hampshire	#Missing	#Missing	#Missing	#Missing	#Missing	#Missing	#Missing	#Missing	#Missing	#Missing
29		California	188	185	191	185	199	231	241	268	205	223
30		Oregon	174	165	161	152	124	125	123	119	132	137

Select *Undo* so we can explore some other member filtering options. Go back to the Member Selection for product. Choose the drop down option for Dimension and note you can select the members for all of the dimensions in the POV. Go ahead and select

Scenario dimension. Choose the *Base members* of Scenario and move them into the Selection section:

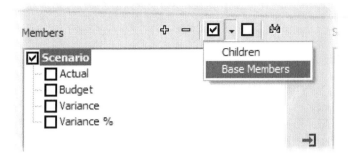

Next choose the Measures dimension. Select the binoculars icon and search for the member beginning with the letters "Sal*":

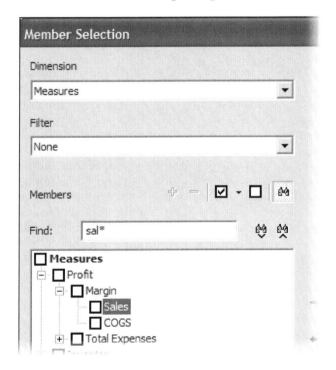

Use the * as a wildcard when searching in Member Selection.

Tip!

Check *Sales* and move it over to the Selection section. Lastly, let's go back to the Product dimension. In the filter drop down, select *Generation*. Type in or select *2* as the Generation:

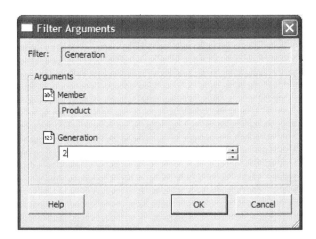

Move the Gen2 products in to the Selection section:

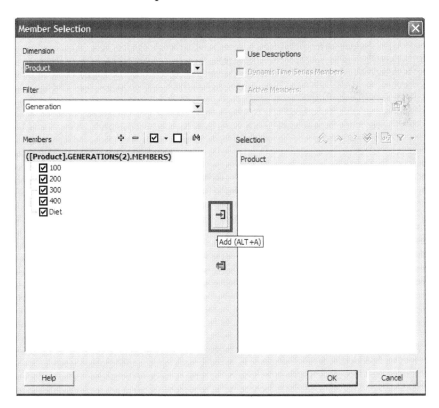

Click *OK* and check out your new member selection lists. So in summary, there are many ways to filter members in your dimensions for reporting and analysis. Remembering your Essbase terminology and knowing the hierarchies will be important in effectively using Member Selection. You can filter by:

- Children
- Descendants
- Level
- Generation
- Attribute
- UDA
- Subset (which is really just another way to filter by attribute)
- Search using wildcards

For any member, you can choose the base members (or level zero members underneath or the children).

Dynamic Time Series

What if the year wasn't complete and we only had data through May? Start by blanking out the cells in row 1 to the right of column G (leaving only the months from January to May). How do we get a year-to-date total column? We could add a total column to the right of column F to add January through May, but Essbase can do this work for us (Do we have to work anymore with Essbase? Oh right, time can now be spent actually analyzing the data versus getting the data.)

Select cell G1 in your spreadsheet (to the right of May) and open the Member Selection box. The Year dimension should appear in the drop-down. Most every Essbase database has a time dimension. In Sample.Basic, that dimension is called Year. When the time dimension for a given database is selected (Year, for us), an extra view method called *Dynamic Time Series* becomes available in the top-right. Go ahead and select it.

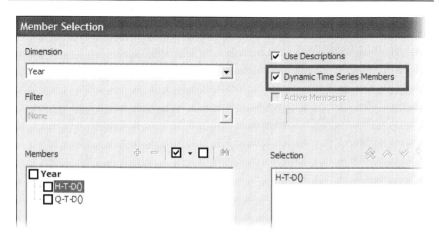

Dynamic Time Series means that Essbase will take and dynamically add up time periods up to whatever period you specify just as if that member was stored in the outline. For instance, if you ask for Q-T-D (Q-T-D is short for Quarter-To-Date) through May, Essbase will total the data for April and May (since those are the months in the quarter containing May) and put them into a Q-T-D member. This member can then be pivoted and for the most part treated just like a stored member.

Sample.Basic has two Dynamic Time Series members (often abbreviated as "DTS members"): Q-T-D and H-T-D. H-T-D stands for History-To-Date. Other common DTS members include Y-T-D (Year-To-Date), M-T-D (Month-To-Date), and W-T-D (Week-To-Date). Since we want January through May to be totaled for us, select H-T-D and add it to the right side.

Notice that below H-T-D has no month specified – H-T-D(). To select the month, click the DTS icon near the Selection section and choose the to-date month:

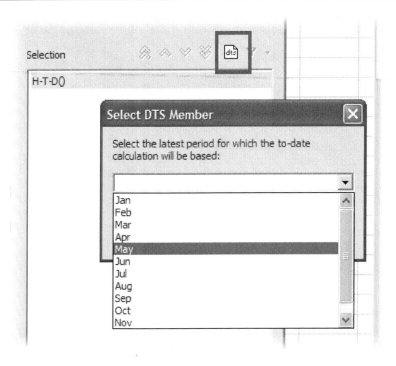

Choose *May*, click *OK*, and then click *OK* again. H-T-D(May) should now be typed into your spreadsheet. Choose *Refresh* and you should see:

	A	B	C	D	E	F	G	
1		Jan	Feb	Mar	Apr	May	H-T-D(May)	Ju
2	Market	2355	2329	2364	2442	2571	12061	29
3	Massachusetts	367	340	366	397	434	1904	
4	New York	262	245	259	276	295	1337	
5	Florida	135	134	141	171	178	759	
6	Connecticut	115	121	114	107	98	555	
7	New Hampshire	45	48	55	60	66	274	

Note!

You can also type in DTS members directly. To specify a specific month, put it in parentheses after the member. For instance to get Q-T-D through March, type in Q-T-D(Mar). There is no space between the member and the parenthesis.

Note!

Your Essbase administrator enables D-T-S.

Substitution Variables

Another retrieval alternative available to you, if your administrator has defined them, is substitution variables. These objects are created and managed by the Essbase administrator to help in Essbase maintenance as well as reporting (that's the part you care about). The variable is a holding place for information that changes on a periodic basis and used in a number of places. Current month, current year, prior year are all examples of common substitution variables. Beginning in 11.1.1.1, Smart View supports Substitution Variables. To use a substitution variable, simply type an & in front of the variable name in the spreadsheet where you'd like to display the member:

Click *Refresh* and the member assigned to the variable will display. So now when Lumbergh requests that TPS report, you can type in the substitution variable and immediately refresh the report. Great.

Attribute Dimensions

All the analysis of Sample.Basic up to this point has been done using five dimensions. There are five other dimensions in Sample.Basic that we could be using but to this point, we've been ignoring them. These dimensions are known as "Attribute Dimensions" and they are alternate ways of summarizing our base (sometimes called "standard" or "stored") dimensions. Thankfully we are covering these dimensions now because since you wow'ed Lumbergh with the detailed state analysis, he has just requested an additional analysis by Caffeinated products. He is sure this will require work over the weekend. "I'm also going to need you to come in on Sunday too."

Note! Unlike base dimensions, the totals for attribute dimensions are not pre-calculated in Essbase. As such, retrieval of attribute dimensions will often be slower as Essbase dynamically calculates the results.

Sample.Basic has five attribute dimensions: Caffeinated, Ounces, Pkg Type, Intro Date, and Population. The first four of these are alternate ways of rolling up the Product dimension. Population is an alternate way of rolling up the Market dimension. As an example, let's limit the report we just made to only caffeinated drinks.

Insert a row at the beginning of your spreadsheet. Select cell B1 (which should be blank) and type *"Caffeinated"* in the cell. Click *Refresh*.

	A	B	C	D	E	F	G
1		Caffeinated					
2		Jan	Feb	Mar	Apr	May	H-T-D(May)
3	Market	2355	2329	2364	2442	2571	12061
4	Massachusetts	367	340	366	397	434	1904
5	New York	262	245	259	276	295	1337
6	Florida	135	134	141	171	178	759
7	Connecticut	115	121	114	107	98	555

Since we haven't been getting much sleep lately, let's focus just on Caffeinated products. To keep your spreadsheet a bit simpler, *Keep only* on Jan and make sure the Product dimension is set to "Products". *Zoom in* to Caffeinated and you should see the data broken up by Caffeinated True and Caffeinated False.

	A	B	C	D
1		Caffeinated_True	Caffeinated_False	Caffeinated
2		Jan	Jan	Jan
3	Market	5563	2461	8024
4	Massachusetts	361	158	519
5	New York	88	424	512
6	Florida	280	56	336
7	Connecticut	239	82	321
8	New Hampshire	11	33	44
9	California	694	340	1034
10	Oregon	264	180	444
11	Washington	244	161	405

Once an attribute has been brought into your spreadsheet, it is then available for use in Member Selection. Select *Undo* to go back one step (or *Zoom out* on Caffeinated True) to get back to Caffeinated. Select Caffeinated and choose *Member Selection.* All of the same member selection options are available for Attribute dimensions (that are applicable; e.g. UDAs and Attributes are not available for attribute dimensions):

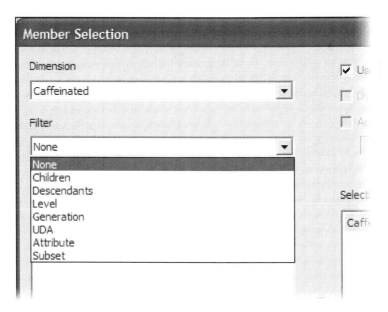

Select Caffeinated True and click *OK*.

Add a member of another attribute dimension into your report and refresh.

Try It!

Notice that in Massachusetts (another member you'd be very likely to misspell if not for Member Selection), out of seven caffeinated products that TBC sells, only three are actually sold there.

There's a quick way to figure out which products those are. Select the cell containing Massachusetts and choose *Keep Only*. Highlight the Caffeinated_True member and choose *Zoom In* or just double click on Caffeinated_True.

	A	B	C	D	E	
1				Sum	Count	Avg.
2				Jan	Jan	Jan
3	Caffeinated_True	Cola	Massachusetts	367	1	
4		Old Fashioned	Massachusetts	-23	1	
5		Dark Cream	Massachusetts	17	1	
6		Product	Massachusetts	361	3	120

Your spreadsheet might look slightly different depending on what you have set in your Options, but you can now easily tell that the only caffeinated products sold in Massachusetts are Cola, Old Fashioned, and Dark Cream.

You can also use attribute members as a method for filtering members in Member Selection. Select Massachusetts in your current spreadsheet and select *Member Selection*. Choose *Attribute* from the filter drop down. Click on the magnifying glass icon to find the attribute dimension and value for filtering:

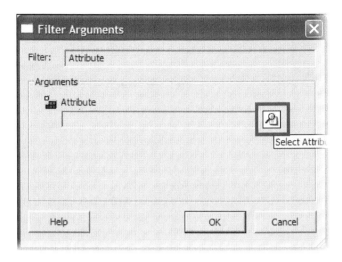

Let's say for example we want to retrieve data for all of the small markets. Select the Population attribute dimension and the Small attribute value. Click the *Add* button:

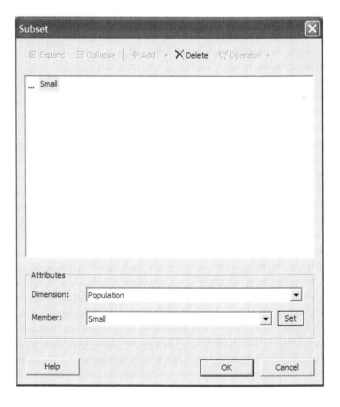

The member list is filtered for all products with the associated attribute value of "Small":

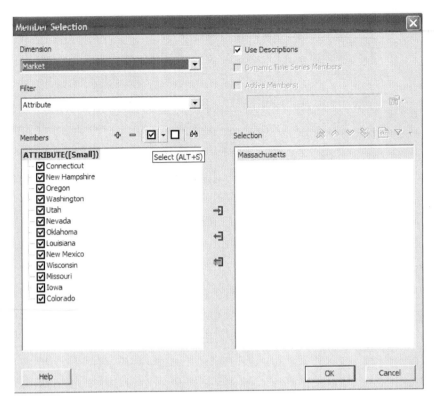

Now that we've covered the regular attributes, let's discuss varying attributes.

Varying Attributes

Did you get the memo? In version 11 Essbase can now handle varying attributes (attributes that may vary over one or more dimensions). For example, your administrator may have created an attribute for Job Status assigned to the Employee dimension. An employee may change their status over the course of the year (e.g. Active to Sabbatical). In a regular attribute dimension when we try to report on the job status, we only see the current assigned status assigned to the employee. So it looks like the employee has spent the whole year on sabbatical when in reality he was active for the first three months of the year. Varying attributes allow you to analyze based on "reality" or based on a historical point in time.

Oh no. Lumbergh is back with a new report requirement. "Yeah. The consultants are coming tomorrow. I'm going to need a sales report by Sales Manager so we can understand everyone's performance. Thankfully your Essbase administrator set up the Sales Manager attribute as a varying attribute dimension because the products managed can vary over time. You want to get this right; peoples jobs are at risk!

Note!

The following examples use a modified version of Sample.Basic which includes varying attributes. (The installed samples do not include varying attributes.) To obtain a copy of this outline and sample data, please email info@interrel.com. Your administrator can take these objects and create another sample application for you.

In this example, a Sales Manager has been assigned to each product. By using all of the techniques we've covered so far, create the following worksheet (Bob and Larry are level 0 members of the Sales Manager varying attribute dimension):

	A	B	C	D	E	F	G	H	I	J	K	L	M	N	
1			Jan	Feb	Mar	Apr	May	Jun	Jul	Aug	Sep	Oct	Nov	Dec	Y
2			Sales	Sales	Sales	Sales	Sales	Sales	Sales	Sales	Sales	Sales	Sales	Sales	S
3	100-10	Bob	4860	4821	4904	5048	#Invalid	#Invalid	#Invalid	#Invalid	#Invalid	#Invalid	#Invalid	#Invalid	1
4	100-10	Larry	#Invalid	#Invalid	#Invalid	#Invalid	5252	5748	5959	6014	5325	4902	4817	5174	4
5	100-20	Bob	2372	2433	2471	2588	2628	2741	2929	2724	2404	2365	#Invalid	#Invalid	2
6	100-20	Larry	#Invalid	#Invalid	#Invalid	#Invalid	#Invalid	#Invalid	#Invalid	#Invalid	#Invalid	#Invalid	2311	2503	

In a matter of seconds, you create the report Lumbergh requests. You can see that Bob managed product 100-10 from January through April and then Larry took over product sales in May. For product 100-20, Bob managed from January through October and Larry managed from November through the end of the year. By default, you are viewing reality.

Now pretend you are Bob and you've had two products taken away from you over the year. You're worried about the consultants and want to find out what your sales would have been had you continued to manage product 100-10 and 100-20 through the end of the year. This will help you to decide whether or not to throw the venti latte in your hand at Larry.

So to change the "perspective" on viewing the data select *Hyperion >> Data Perspective.* Choose the *Custom* radio button and select March for the Year dimension (how Sales Manager can vary).

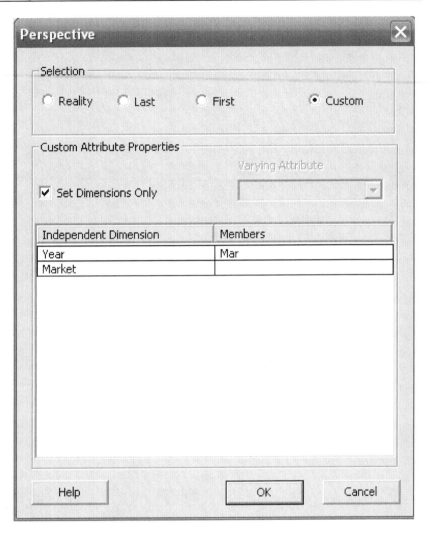

Click *OK* and refresh the data. The view will now display Bob as the Sales Manager for the full year as if it were March (back when life was good and full of cola products to manage). Still pretending that you are Bob, you grab your venti-latte and start looking for Larry.

	A	B	C	D	E	F	G	H	I	J	K	L	M	N	O
1			Jan	Feb	Mar	Apr	May	Jun	Jul	Aug	Sep	Oct	Nov	Dec	Year
2			Sales	Sales	Sales	Sales	Sales	Sales	Sales	Sales	Sales	Sales	Sales	Sales	Sales
3	100-10	Bob	4860	4821	4904	5048	5252	5748	5959	6014	5325	4902	4817	5174	62804
4	100-20	Bob	2372	2433	2471	2588	2628	2741	2929	2724	2404	2365	2311	2503	30469
5															

You can also use varying attributes for member selection as well. For example, Bob wants to pull in a list of all products that he has ever managed. First let's understand the difference in filtering on attributes vs. varying attributes. In the spreadsheet, select the Product dimension and filter the member list for *Attribute*:

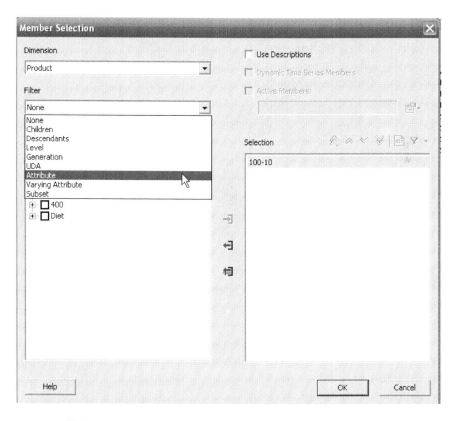

Click the magnifying glass to select the attribute, choosing *Sales Manager*:

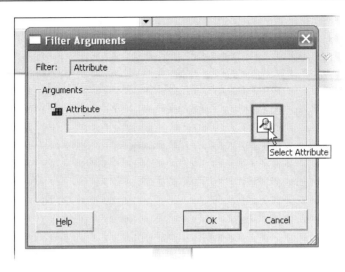

Select Bob (bottom of the dialog box) and click the *Add* button (top of the dialog box):

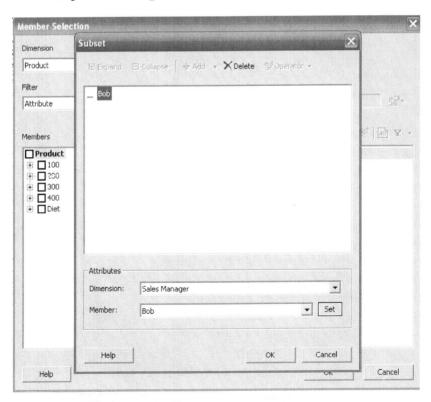

The member selection will filter for any products where Bob was solely the manager. The products where Bob managed for a period of time (but not the entire year) are not displayed. So this won't work for Bob's query requirements.

Now let's filter using the Varying Attribute option. This will only display if you have varying attributes defined for the selected dimension. Select the Member Selection for the Product dimension if necessary. Under Filter, select *Varying Attribute*.

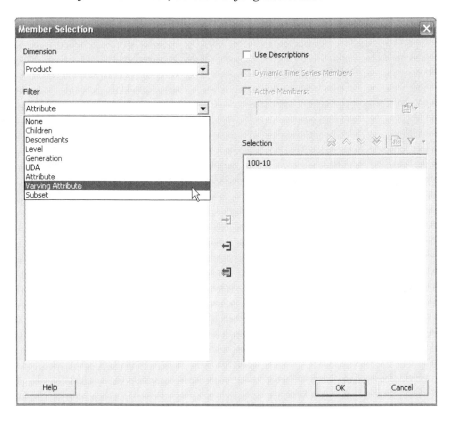

Click the magnifying glass to select the attribute. Choose the ellipses button to choose the varying attribute dimension. Select the Sales Manager attribute dimension (bottom of the dialog box), choose Bob and finally click the *Add* button:

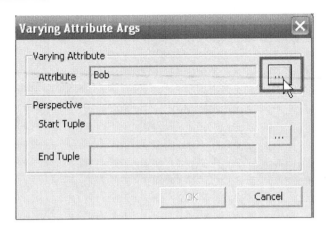

Notice how we jump from top to bottom to top in the Attribute/Subset window.

Note!

Next click on the ellipses button to choose the start tuple (or start of the range) and the end tuple (or end of the range).

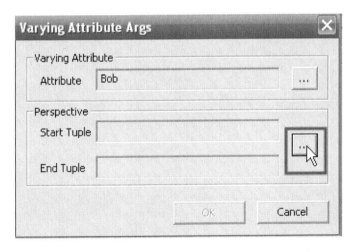

Choose Range to define the range of members. Optionally, you could have chosen Snapshot (filter for a specific member). In this example of the worried employee, choose Jan as the start tuple and Dec as the end tuple. This allows us to see any products that Bob has managed in the months January through December.

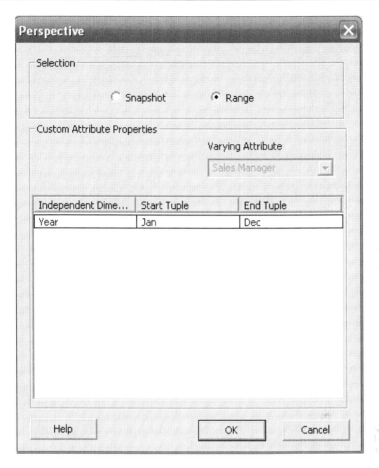

Once you click OK, you should see the following:

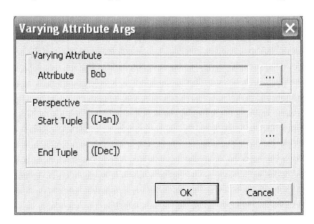

Click OK again (are we ever going to get there?):

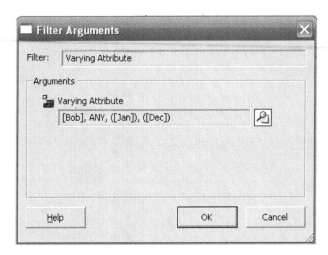

Finally, we see the member list filtering Products that Bob managed throughout the year, even those managed for just a few months.

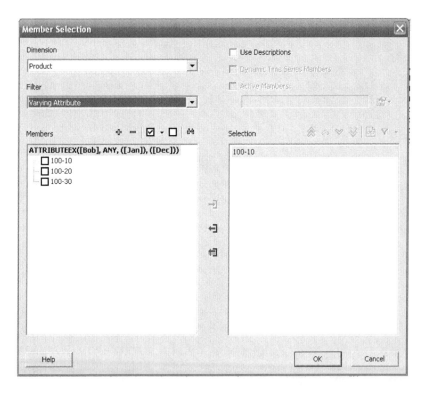

Now you and Bob are fully prepared for the performance review with the consultants. You've pulled the good, the bad, and the ugly for each and every sales manager, using the new Essbase 11 feature, varying attributes, to fully understand how sales varied over other Essbase dimensions. Next let's review another new Essbase 11 feature - text and dates.

Text and Date Lists

At the beginning of this book, you were probably one of those people who often said, "I uh, I don't like my job, and, uh, I don't think I'm gonna go anymore. Not going to quit. I'm just gonna stop going." Now that Essbase has entered your life, things are different now. No working on the weekends for Lumbergh. Plenty of time to organize the sock drawer. Just wait... it gets better. Beginning in 11.1.1.1 Essbase now supports text and date list values (whoo hoo!! Yes. We are certified geeks). It's still not free form text but we finally have the ability to present and analyze non-numeric data:

	A	B	C	D
1		Sales	Customer_Satisfaction_Level	
2	100-10	678	High	
3	200-10	61	Low	
4	200-40	490	High	
5	300-10	483	High	
6	300-20	180	Low	
7	400-10	234	Low	
8	400-20	219	Low	
9	400-30	134	Low	
10	Product	2479	Missing	
11				
12				

The text and date values are created and managed by your administrator. How do you analyze this information? The exact same way that we've been analyzing the numeric data. If you have write access to the text or date list, you can also choose a value from the drop down list and submit it back to the server:

	Sales	Package Type
Cola	40013.2	Bottle
Diet Cola	12640.6	Can
Caffeine Free Cola	6281.6	Can
Colas	58935.4	Bottle
		Can
		Invalid

FormatString

Formatstring is another new feature in Essbase 11.1.1.1 that provides the administrator the ability to format data on the Essbase server. They can add prefixes or suffixes to data values (e.g. adding parentheses for negative values) or convert numbers to text based on defined criteria (e.g. see Variance Level in column G; variance has been translated to a text based value):

	A	B	C	D	E	F	G
1					Market		
2					Sales		
3			Actual	Budget	Variance	Variance %	Variance level
4	100-10	Year	62824	67190	-4366	-6.50	Low
5	100-20	Year	30469	33520	-3051	-9.10	Low
6	100-30	Year	12841	13600	-759	-5.58	Low
7	100	Year	106134	114310	-8176	-7.15	Low
8	200-10	Year	41537	42300	-763	-1.80	Low
9	200-20	Year	38240	37860	380	1.00	Low
10	200-30	Year	17559	15270	2289	14.99	High
11	200-40	Year	11750	11310	440	3.89	Low
12	200	Year	109086	106740	2346	2.20	Low
13	300-10	Year	46956	39150	7806	19.94	Very High
14	300-20	Year	17480	14160	3320	23.45	Very High
15	300-30	Year	36969	31920	5049	15.82	Very High
16	300	Year	101405	85230	16175	18.98	Very High
17	400	Year	84230	66800	17430	26.09	Very High
18	Diet	Year	105678	103300	2378	2.30	Low
19	Product	Year	400855	373080	27775	7.44	Medium level

In order to see the Formatstring values, make sure to check the option *Format String* under *Options* on the Display tab:

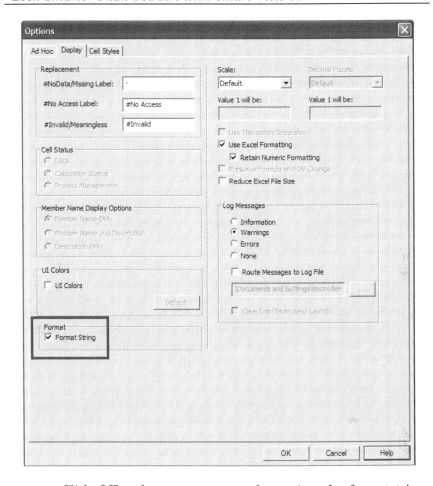

Click *OK* and you are now ready to view the formatstring data. If you'd like to see the underlying numbers that support the formatstring logic, simply uncheck this box.

Report and analysis requests are now overflowing from Lumbergh. Despite his repeated question "Is this good for the company", you are sure he is just trying to somehow make you work the weekend. But with Essbase at your side, you are an invincible analyzing machine and we'll show you more tools to quickly create queries: Query Designer, Point of Views and Copy/Paste Data Points.

INTRODUCTION TO QUERY DESIGNER

In Smart View 9.3, a new query designer was introduced to help users create queries against Essbase. This feature is especially helpful when you already know the layout for your report as you define the layout in one single step (vs. drilling, zooming, and member selecting). You create a cross dimensional layout for the query and then add filters for properties like UDAs, attributes or filters for data. You can also execute free form MDX query in the Smart View Query Designer.

Some restrictions should be considered during the design of queries in Query Designer:

- Formulas are not supported
- Asymmetric reports are not supported
- Comments are not supported on the query sheet; only member names are supported
- Blank rows or columns are not supported
- Alias tables cannot be changed
- Ad Hoc actions, such as zoom in and out, keep and remove only, and double-click are not supported

However, after design is complete and you've run the query, these features are available for use.

To create a query in the Smart View Query Designer, connect to *Sample.Basic.* Select *Hyperion >> Query >> Query Designer* or click the *Query Designer* button on the Hyperion ribbon:

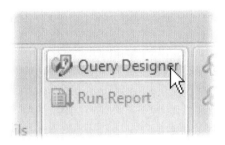

The Query Designer will display:

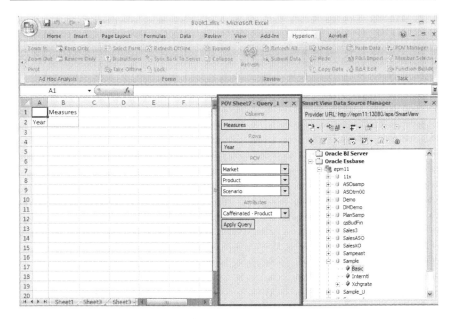

Using the Query Designer, first organize your layout by dragging dimensions to the desired rows, columns and POVs. Next use member selection to select the specific members for each dimension just as you learned in the previous section. Don't forget that in the Member Selection window, you can add member filters by the following:

- Children
- Descendants
- Level
- Generation
- UDA
- Attribute
- Subset of attribute dimensions to create conditional expressions

In this example, let's define the layout for our query with the four quarters across our columns, children of Margin and Margin in the rows, and Actual, Markets, "100" in the POV:

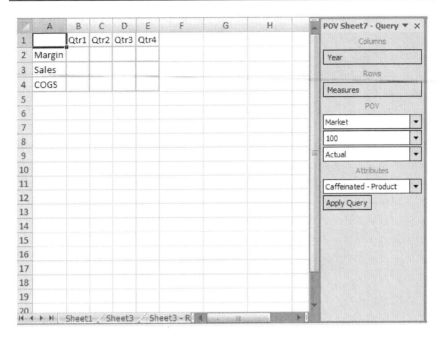

To run the report, select *Hyperion >> Query >> Run Report* or click on the POV toolbar or click the *Apply Query* button. The query will process and display:

	A	B	C	D	E	F	G
1		Qtr1	Qtr2	Qtr3	Qtr4		
2	Margin	14378	15574	16383	14451		
3	Sales	25048	27187	28544	25355		
4	COGS	10670	11613	12161	10904		
5							
6							
7							
8							

You can toggle back to the query designer by selecting the *Query Designer* button.

If you want to extract a query from an existing report so that you can more easily modify its definition or apply a data filter, simply select the *Query Designer* button and modify the query as needed. Select *Run Report* or *Apply Query* after the modifications have been made:

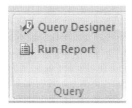

Create your own a query using Query Designer for Sample.Basic. Show it to all of your friends (if you still have friends).

Try It!

    To save a query, simply save the Excel spreadsheet. You can share the Excel spreadsheet and the query design with other users.

    As mentioned earlier, one benefit of the Query Designer is that you can apply data filters. Let's walk through an example. To apply a data filter, select *Hyperion >> Data Filter*. Under Count, select Top or Bottom and specify a number. Under Set, select the Dimension, and in the Member Selection dialog box, select a row member for ranking, and click *OK* to return to the Data Filter dialog box. Under Value, select the Dimension, and in the Member Selection dialog box, select a column member to run the ranking against, and click OK to return to the Data Filter dialog box. Click *OK* when you are done:

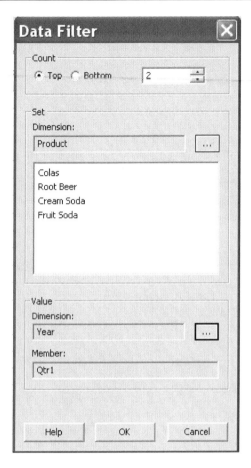

Select *Run Report*. A MDX query that represents your data filtering settings is inserted into the grid.

Note!

MDX is a standard query language for Essbase databases (sort of like SQL for relational databases).

Let us consider the following example: TopCount({ [Qtr3] }, 10, [Measures].[Profit]) which returns the top 2 most profitable products in quarter 3:

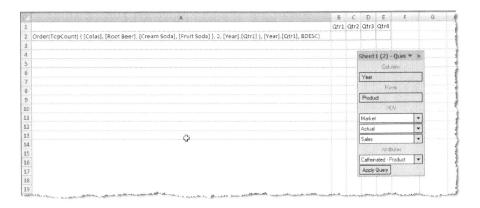

The result would look like the following:

	A	B	C	D	E	F	G	H
1		Qtr1	Qtr2	Qtr3	Qtr4			
2	Root Beer	26.62700126	27.4010013	27.94200133	27.11600129			
3	Colas	25.04800119	27.18700129	28.54400136	25.3550012			

So when would I use the Query Designer vs. a regular adhoc query? The following table illustrates a comparison of the two options:

	Regular Adhoc Query	*Query Designer*
Define the POV, Rows, and Columns	Multiple steps	One step
Apply Member filters	Y	Y
Apply Data filters	N	Y
You know the query definition at the beginning	Good	Best
You've drilled into a query and want	Good	Best

	Regular Adhoc Query	*Query Designer*
to get back to the original starting point		
Allows free form MDX	N	Y
Save queries using Excel save functionality	Y	Y
Copy across worksheets	Y	Y

POINT OF VIEWS

Smart View provides the ability to utilize point of views across spreadsheets. A point of view is the default starting point for each dimension for a database connection. POVs are used primarily with default starting points for adhoc analysis and in the background for data points (data points will be covered in a later section).

Before we move into the details, we want to advise caution when using point of views; while in many cases you will be able to use them with no problems, they can be **Note!** unpredictable or buggy at times.

If you are performing adhoc analysis and want to leverage a saved POV, you must open an unconnected worksheet. You can copy a saved POV to a blank worksheet. Select *Refresh* and the POV will be applied to the query. You can copy POVs to different spreadsheets but for those that already have queried grids, the POV will have no effect. Once you start using the grid, you can no longer make changes with the POV Manager.

For example, you are the sales manager for the East region for Diet Cola products so you might want your POV to be the following:

Market: East
Scenario: Actual
Products: Diet Colas
Accounts: Sales

Do you have to reference every dimension in your POV? No, you can pick and choose the dimensions that are applicable for your POV. Can you reference more than one member for a single dimension in a POV? No, you can only choose one member for each dimension.

You can edit POVs, save POVs, copy and paste POVs between worksheets as well as delete POVs. You can share POVs with users as long as their database connections are identical to your database connections (in version 11 this is automatically done; in System 9, communication in naming conventions for database connections are important).

By default the POV will reference the top member of every dimension. To edit a POV, select *Hyperion >> POV Manager*. Expand to view the Active POV:

 A POV is tied to a database connection.
Note!

Make sure the Query Designer is closed when you want to work with the POV Manager. If the Query Designer is open, the POV Manager option is grayed out.

Let's edit the POV for our East sales manager. Select the dimension by double clicking in each dimension in the POV Manager and the Member Selection window will display. Choose the desired members for each dimension (in our case, East, Diet Colas, and Sales).

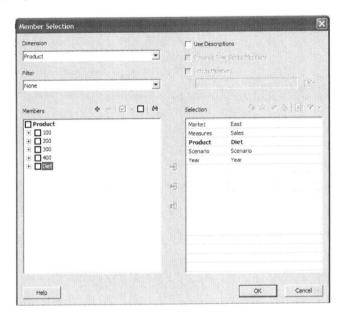

Once you've selected all of the desired members, your POV Manager should look like the following:

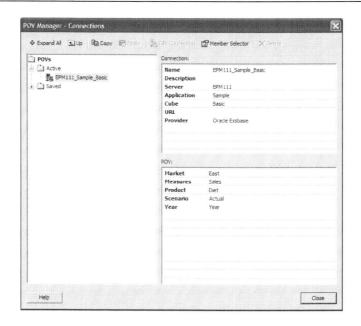

Now refresh your existing report or query. Nothing happened, right? Yes, unfortunately once you've retrieved data the POV becomes useless in adhoc analysis or existing grids in Excel. POVs provide the real value in starting point analysis (and in use of data points covered in just a bit).

Let's copy this POV to a blank worksheet. To copy and paste a point of view, select *Hyperion >> POV Manager*. From the Active folder, select the Active application connection. Select the members for the POV and save the workbook. Click *Copy:*

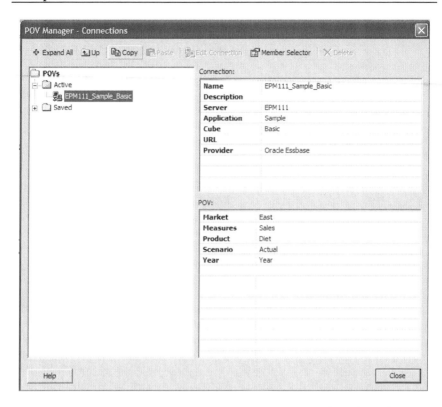

Expand the Saved folder to select the workbook and blank worksheet into which you want to paste the POV. Click *Paste*:

Tip!

You can also drag and drop POVs within the POV Manager.

Navigate to the worksheet. Activate the database connection if necessary. Select *Hyperion >> Refresh* and you should see the following:

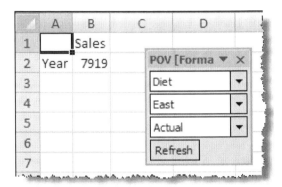

Optionally, to copy a saved POV from another workbook, open the workbook and select the saved POV. Copy and paste the source POV to the target worksheet in the Saved folder:

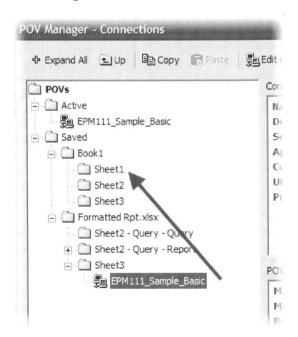

To close the POV Manager, click *Close*.

When you share workbooks, saved POVs help ensure that everyone is looking at the same data. Saved POVs are referenced with the data source name of the computer on which they were saved. So that means you have to have the same data source name for the application with the same URL. If the connection information is different, you can't paste the active POV into the worksheet for a different user.

You can print POV members in the headers and footers section of your Excel spreadsheet. In Excel, navigate to Page Setup. Under Headers/Footers, choose *Custom Header* or *Custom Footer*. Type in the statement POV:{} to pull in the current POV selections:

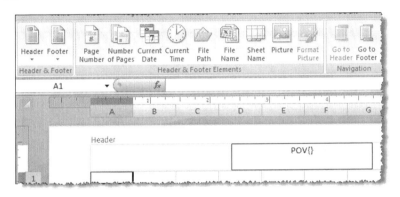

Click *OK* and *OK* to confirm changes and the resulting header (or footer) will display:

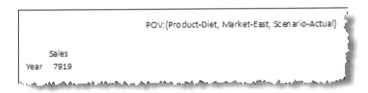

COPY DATA POINTS

"What's happening? Yeah. I'm gonna need that analysis you did on Margin and Profit by Ounces in Word format. And I may need an updated version after close. Is that going to be a problem? No? OK. That would be terrific. By the end of the day," says Lumbergh with a wish-I-could-wipe-that-grin-off-your-face smirk. Fortunately for you, this request isn't a problem. One of the coolest features in Smart View is the copy and paste data points feature. Available in 9.3, this feature allows you to copy data points from spreadsheet to spreadsheet, spreadsheet to Word document, PowerPoint to spreadsheet, and more. What's the coolest is that the data points remained linked to the database (yes, we are still geeks!) so if the underlying data changes, you can just refresh the copied data points.

Create the following spreadsheet. To copy and paste data points, select the grid to copy in Excel:

	A	B	C	D	E	F	G	H
1			Qtr1	Qtr1	Qtr1	Qtr1		
2			Actual	Budget	Variance	Variance %		
3	Ounces	Margin	48106	51540	-3434	-6.662786185		
4	Ounces	Total Expenses	28240	20960	-7280	-34.73282443		
5	Ounces	Profit	19866	30580	-10714	-35.03597122		
6								
7								
8								
9								

[Book1]Sh ▼ ×
Product ▼
Market ▼
Refresh

Select *Copy Data* from the Hyperion ribbon:

Select the new spreadsheet and select *Paste Data*. The copied grid will be pasted into the spreadsheet:

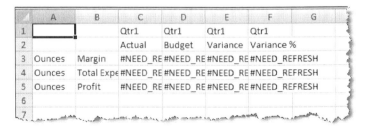

	A	B	C	D	E	F	G
1			Qtr1	Qtr1	Qtr1	Qtr1	
2			Actual	Budget	Variance	Variance %	
3	Ounces	Margin	#NEED_RE	#NEED_RE	#NEED_RE	#NEED_REFRESH	
4	Ounces	Total Expe	#NEED_RE	#NEED_RE	#NEED_RE	#NEED_REFRESH	
5	Ounces	Profit	#NEED_RE	#NEED_RE	#NEED_RE	#NEED_REFRESH	
6							
7							

Click *Refresh* to refresh the data points. What are copied are data points, not a query (use query designer to do that). Here you are copying individual data points across Microsoft products. Note what is stored in each individual cell (or data point) is linked information about the data point (server, application, cube / database, member intersection for all dimensions and alias table):

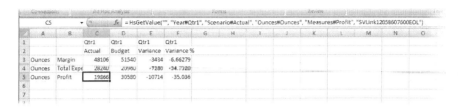

 Mouse over a data point to see the connection information.
Note!

That's good and all but what about Word or PowerPoint? You have this new request for Lumbergh to fill. The real benefit of copying data points is using this feature with Word and PowerPoint. Simply open a Word or PowerPoint document and choose *Paste Data* from the Hyperion ribbon:

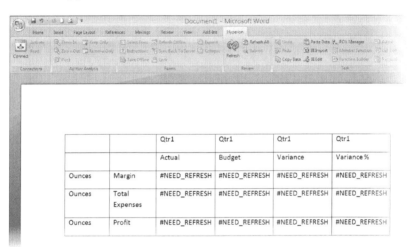

After pasting the data points into Word (or PowerPoint), hit *Refresh* to pull in the current data values. Wala! Essbase numbers in a Word document (can't nobody hold you down, including Lumbergh!).

So what if you are looking at Essbase data in Word or PowerPoint and you want to further analyze that data set? Simple. Select the desired data point and click the *Visualize in Excel* button on the Hyperion ribbon (or *Hyperion >> Linked >> Visualize in Excel*) to pull the grid back into Excel where you can perform further analytics:

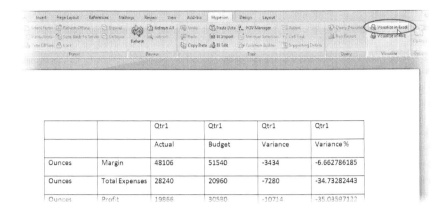

		Qtr1	Qtr1	Qtr1	Qtr1
		Actual	Budget	Variance	Variance %
Ounces	Margin	48106	51540	-3434	-6.662786185
Ounces	Total Expenses	28240	20960	-7280	-34.73282443
Ounces	Profit	19866	30580	-10714	-35.03597122

This step brings you to a linked query in Excel:

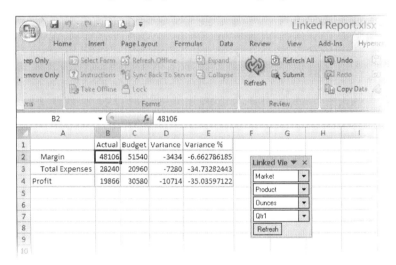

Copy data points between a spreadsheet and a Word document. Change the underlying data and refresh the Word document.

Try It!

Do you have to copy the full grid? Nope, you can just copy a single data point (the data).

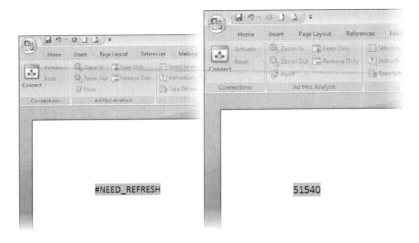

Data points in Office allow you to easily create multi-source reports and spreadsheets (more on how to do this in a later section). A single Excel spreadsheet or Word document can contain data points from different Essbase databases, giving you the flexibility to pull together information from across your Essbase databases. The following example shows one worksheet with data points from both Sample.Basic and Sample.Interntl databases:

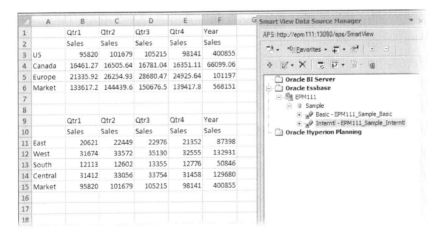

Before we conclude our Power User chapter, we need to revisit one last "power" topic: Managing Connections.

MANAGE CONNECTIONS

You've now connected to the Sample.Basic database several times. Pretty straight forward, right? Yes, in the Essbase world, life is gloriously simple but is there more (should we settle or embrace change)? Before we digress into life lessons, let's focus and say yes, there are some additional connection features that can help you in your Essbase reporting and analysis process. Also many of you may be using Smart View for Planning, Financial Management or other BI / EPM tools so let us expand on our connecting capabilities.

Three types of connections exist in the Oracle EPM and BI environment: Common Provider Connections, Independent Provider Connections and Simulation & Forecasting Workbooks.

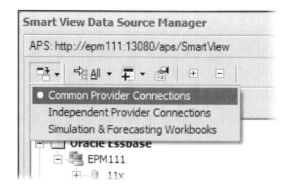

Common Provider Connections are available for Essbase, Planning and OBIEE sources. These connections leverage a single common provider service (hence, the name Common Provider Connections) and are managed using the Data Source Manager. Independent Provider Connections are used for Financial Management, Enterprise, Reporting and Analysis modules like Financial Reporting, Web Analysis, and Interactive Reporting. Independent Provider Connections do not leverage the common provider services. They connect directly to the application via a URL or Oracle Hyperion Shared Services. Simulation & Forecasting Workbooks connections are used for Oracle Crystal Ball sources.

Note!

We believe eventually all sources will be brought into the Smart View Common Provider Services.

Since Essbase uses the Common Provider Services, we'll focus there. One of the very first things we did back in the beginning of the book (we've come a long way, baby) was to show all of the connections (which shows all available connections). Two other options exist for your common provider connections: Pre-Defined and Favorites.

Pre-defined connections will list all data sources that have been defined by the Administrator. Favorites connections will list sources that you've picked as a "favorite".

Adding a Favorite Connection

To add a favorite or if you are the administrator, a predefined connection in the Smart View Data Source Manager, right click on the desired cube and choose *Add To Favorites* or *Add To Pre-defined:*

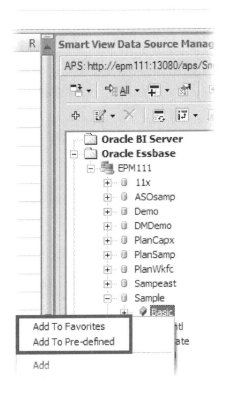

Follow along with us and right click on Sample.Basic and select *Add To Favorites*. Next change the connection view from *All* to *Favorites:*

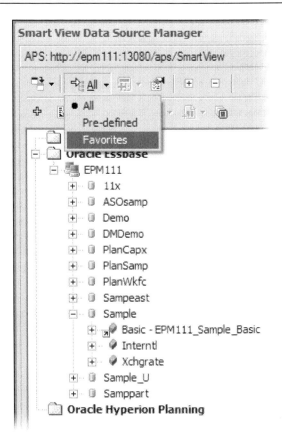

Expand through the Essbase tree and notice the data source list is now filtered, only displaying the Sample.Basic database (notice the icon changed from a blue cube to a pink cube with a new name – *server_application_database*):

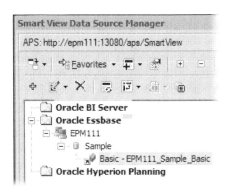

Most importantly, adding the Essbase connection as a favorite allows you to use the *Activate* option for your spreadsheets. Why is this important you may ask? This is how you can tell the cube for which you are connected. You can also use this mechanism for connecting report templates where you don't want to *Adhoc Analyze*. Select the *Activate* drop down and note the checked connection:

If you need to report and analyze against an Essbase database, add it as a Favorite.

Tip!

Assuming you are already in Excel and connected to the Data Source Manager for another spreadsheet, create a new worksheet and type in the following: Cell B1 "Sales", Cell A2 " Actual:

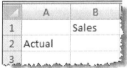

From the Hyperion ribbon, select *Activate* and choose the Sample.Basic connection:

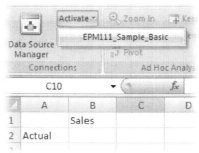

Click *Refresh* and note the data is immediately retrieved from the source.

Tip!

If you have upgraded from an earlier Smart View version, you can migrate your existing Essbase connections to your Favorites. Did you add your Essbase cubes as Favorites yet?

We've now taken you through the advanced analytics portion of the book, analyzing data at the speed of light (well almost the speed of light). We'll next turn our attention to dynamic formatted reporting with Smart View and Essbase.

Chapter 5:
Create Formatted Reports

"Did you see the memo about this? We're going to need detailed formatting on all of the reports before they go out. So if you could go ahead and try to remember to do that from now on, that'd be great. All right!" Before you throw this book at Lumbergh's head (again), let us learn the ins and outs of formatting with Smart View. We'll first cover Excel formatting and the seven steps to creating your formatted report. We'll conclude this chapter with a discussion on two other formatting options: capture formatting and cell styles. In the next chapter, we'll show you more reporting capabilities with Smart Slices and Report Designer, new features in version 11 (although formatting information covered in this chapter also applies to Report Designer). Trust us, formatting won't be a problem any longer.

USE EXCEL FORMATTING

Everything we've done up to this point has been fairly ad hoc and formatting has been kept to a minimum. One of the reasons we're using Excel to display our data is that it's a great place to pretty up boring numbers (or as we used to say back on the farm: "making 'em look fancy"). Essbase will still be used as the source of the data, but Excel will provide all of our formatting.

Using what you've learned so far, create the following P&L statement for TBC:

	A	B	C	D	E	F
1		Actual	Budget		POV [Book1 ▼ ✕	
2	Sales	400855	373080		Product ▼	
3	COGS	179336	158940		Market ▼	
4	Margin	221519	214140		Year ▼	
5	Marketing	66237	49520		Refresh	
6	Payroll	48747	35240			
7	Misc	1013	-			
8	Total Expenses	115997	84760			
9	Profit	105522	129380			

We now have a P&L statement but it doesn't look that great. What we really need to do is apply some formatting to this spreadsheet.

Enable Excel Formatting

We are in Excel so we can use all the power that is Microsoft for formatting our spreadsheets. Before you start formatting with Excel, select *Options* and choose the *Display* tab.

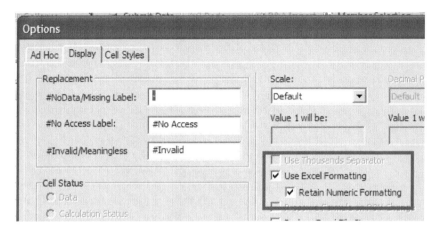

Use this tab to define how you want missing data and "no access" cells to display. Define scale and decimal places for the spreadsheet as well as define the thousands separator. Most importantly check *Use Excel Formatting* if you want to save any formatting defined in Microsoft Excel (and disable the use of Cell Styles; we'll cover cell styles in just a moment).

Check the box to *Use Excel Formatting* along with *Retain Numeric Formatting* (this new option in 11.1.1.1 will retain number formatting even as you drill into dimensions – cool). Click *OK* and you're ready. So what are you waiting for? Get formatting. Format your sheet to look like the following using normal Excel formatting options:

	A	B	C	D	E	F
1		**Actual**	**Budget**			
2	Sales	$ 400,855	$ 373,080		POV [Book1 ▼ ×	
3	COGS	$ 179,336	$ 158,940		Product ▼	
4	*Margin*	*$ 221,519*	*$ 214,140*		Market ▼	
5	Marketing	$ 66,237	$ 49,520		Year ▼	
6	Payroll	$ 48,747	$ 35,240			
7	Misc	$ 1,013	-		Refresh	
8	*Total Expenses*	*$ 115,997*	*$ 84,760*			
9	**Profit**	**$ 105,522**	**$ 129,380**			

Click the *Refresh* button and notice the formatting remains. Save this report. Now drag Year into the columns. Oh no! What happened to my formatting?

	A	B	C	D	E	F
1		Year				
2		Actual	Budget		POV [Book1 ▼ ×	
3	Sales	400855	373080		Product ▼	
4	COGS	179336	158940		Market ▼	
5	Margin	221519	214140		Refresh	
6	Marketing	66237	49520			
7	Payroll	48747	35240			
8	Misc	1013	-			
9	Total Expenses	115997	84760			
10	Profit	105522	129380			
11						

If you change the grid layout by adding, removing or moving dimensions or if you drill into a report, you can probably count on some formatting issues.

Let's now look at those handy 7 steps to creating a report to address this issue.

7 STEPS TO A FORMATTED REPORT

The secret to creating a formatted report (sometimes called a "template") is to use Essbase to get all of your data before you add any formatting. In general, there are seven steps to creating a formatted report:

1. Define your query in Query Designer.
2. Run the query.

3. Move the members.
4. Add any text descriptions.
5. Insert Excel formulas.
6. Apply formatting.
7. Save.

Step 1: Define the Query in Query Designer

Let's say we want to make a fairly simple Profit and Loss Statement. (Considering we'll be using Sample.Basic, it's going to have to be pretty darned simple.) Open a new Excel spreadsheet and connect to the database. If you are already connected simply activate the connection for your new spreadsheet:

Launch the Query Designer and define the following query. Move Product to the columns section but only select Product. Ditto for Market. Move Scenario to the columns section but only select Actual. Move Year to the columns section (make sure Year is last):

Move Measures to the rows and select the following members for the report (in the order shown below):

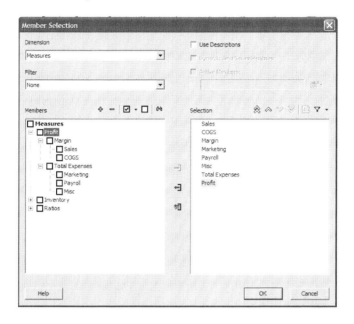

Couldn't you have used the filter for descendants of Profit?

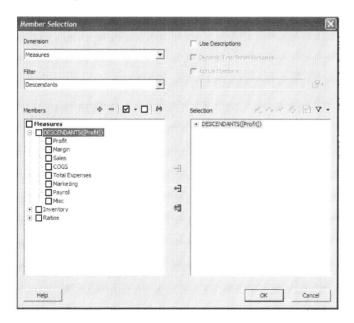

Yes, but the order of the members would have been a bit backwards. The display order of the descendants filter will follow the outline definition from top to bottom so Profit would have been first with Margin second, Sales, etc.

Our last step in the query definition is to select the children of Year:

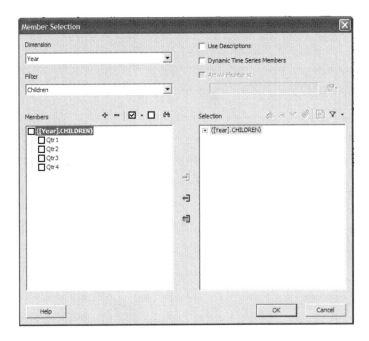

Your query should look like the following:

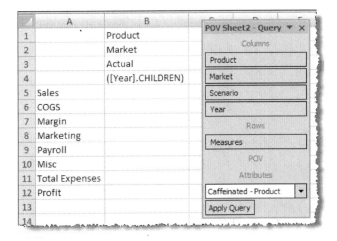

Tip!

Did you know that you can pick up and move around the Query Designer and the Data Source Manager windows? Try it! Select the Window title and move it to another place in the spreadsheet. Then move it back again to the right side of your screen.

Step 2: Run the Query

Click *Apply Query* to run the query and your spreadsheet should look like the following:

	A	B	C	D	E
1		Product			
2		Market			
3		Actual			
4		Qtr1	Qtr2	Qtr3	Qtr4
5	Sales	95820	101679	105215	98141
6	COGS	42877	45362	47343	43754
7	Margin	52943	56317	57872	54387
8	Marketing	15839	16716	17522	16160
9	Payroll	12168	12243	12168	12168
10	Misc	233	251	270	259
11	Total Expenses	28240	29210	29960	28587
12	Profit	24703	27107	27912	25800

If your spreadsheet doesn't look quite like this one, make sure your Essbase display Options are set to indent sub-items and automatically adjust columns.

Tip!

Do I have to use the Query Designer? Nope, you can create the layout in the spreadsheet by typing in member names, drilling, and member selection just as we did at the beginning of the book. Your choice.

Step 3: Move Members

Since this is the data we want to see on our final report, we can proceed on to step two: moving our row, column, and page members around. Our data is a bit cramped at the moment, so let's space it out by inserting some blank rows. Highlight the following rows (by clicking the row number) and select *Insert >> Rows* from the Excel menu. Make your spreadsheet look like the following:

	A	B	C	D	E
1					
2					
3		Product			
4		Market			
5		Actual			
6					
7					
8		Qtr1	Qtr2	Qtr3	Qtr4
9	Sales	95820	101679	105215	98141
10	COGS	42877	45362	47343	43754
11	Margin	52943	56317	57872	54387
12	Marketing	15839	16716	17522	16160
13	Payroll	12168	12243	12168	12168
14	Misc	233	251	270	259
15	Total Expenses	28240	29210	29960	28587
16	Profit	24703	27107	27912	25800
17					

Even though we've inserted a bunch of extra lines, this is still a valid Essbase retrieval. Click *Refresh* to just prove it.

Essbase is quite content to have you move the member names around. Its only requirement is that it needs to encounter a member from every dimension before it sees the first number. Essbase scans a spreadsheet from the left-to-right (cell A1, B1, C1... IV1) and then from top-to-bottom (row 1, row 2, row 3, ... row 65536). As it is reading the first line, the first name it encounters is Product. At this point, it doesn't know if Product applies to the whole page or it's a column member (because theoretically, column C could contain another Product member such as Cola).

Essbase proceeds on to the next cell and sees Market. Since this is from a different dimension, it now knows that this row must contain page members. Essbase calls this a title row. At this point, it's expecting that the next member over will either be blank or a member from another dimension. If the next member over was a different member from either the Product or Market dimension, it would get very confused since it already decided that this was a row of page. An error would appear:

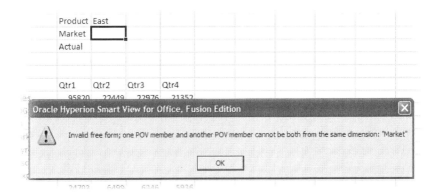

If you ever see this error, look for a row that has multiple dimensions on it that also has multiple members from the same dimension.

We found this problem frequently in the old days of the Excel Add-in. While it is still possible, Smart View provides some structure to limit this issue in some cases.

Note!

Since everything is positioned properly in our current example, Essbase will continue scanning to the right and sees the member Actual. Essbase now has three of the five dimensions specified.

Essbase continues scanning through the rest of row 1 but it encounters nothing but blank cells (and the same occurs with all of rows two, three, and four). In cell B8 it sees the member Qtr1. It recognizes this as being a member of the Year dimension, but like before, it doesn't know yet if row five is a title row or a column row. Looking to the next cell, it sees Qtr2 so it makes the determination that row five is a column row (specifically a row of Year members). Essbase goes on to see Year members in the remaining cells in row five and Essbase becomes very happy.

Moving on to row nine, it sees the member Sales in the first column. Essbase has now identified all five of the base dimensions in Sample.Basic. It now knows the value that should be entered into cell B9 is the intersection of the three page dimensions (Product, Market, Scenario), Qtr1, and Sales.

The general requirement is that Essbase must encounter every dimension before the first number. This is called "the natural order for Essbase." Whenever your retrievals aren't working, look to see if you've violated the natural order rule.

Being practically perfect in every way, our retrieve has none of these problems. Before we conclude step 2, let's move Market to C3, Product to cell C4 and Actual to cell C5. Before you continue to step 3, make sure your retrieve looks like this:

	A	B	C	D	E
1					
2					
3			Market		
4			Product		
5			Actual		
6					
7					
8		Qtr1	Qtr2	Qtr3	Qtr4
9	Sales	95820	101679	105215	98141
10	COGS	42877	45362	47343	43754
11	Margin	52943	56317	57872	54387
12	Marketing	15839	16716	17522	16160
13	Payroll	12168	12243	12168	12168
14	Misc	233	251	270	259
15	Total Expenses	28240	29210	29960	28587
16	Profit	24703	27107	27912	25800

Step 4: Add Text

As Essbase is scanning the sheet, it will often run into names it doesn't recognize. The retrieve will still function even though unknown names are present.

We can use this to our advantage by adding extraneous text to our retrieve knowing that the retrieve will continue to work just fine. Extra text can include header information such as the company or the name of the report. In our case, we're going to add some descriptions to let people know what should be selected in cells B3:B5. Type in the following:

- In cell B3, "Market:"
- In cell B4, "Product:"
- In cell B5, "Scenario:"

The top of your retrieve should now look like this:

	A	B	C
1			
2			
3		Market:	Market
4		Product:	Product
5		Scenario:	Actual
6			

Click *Refresh* and note the text was saved. Next add a title to your report.

At this point you want to finalize the layout. Once we add formulas and formatting, you don't want to make any changes to the layout. If you do, this could mean rework or updates to the formulas and/or formatting. So ask yourself this question: Are you sure this is the final layout? Really sure? If so, then you are ready to move on to the next step.

Step 5: Insert formulas

At times, you may want to add formulas to your report to calculate things that aren't in Essbase. We are of the belief that whenever possible, you should try to add these types of calculations to the Essbase database itself. The main reason is that if you add the calculation to Essbase, anyone else will be guaranteed to calculate that value the exact same way you do. This prevents the embarrassing situation of two people walking into a meeting with different ideas of what Profit as a percent of Sales was last month. This is likely to get one or both people fired (usually, they'll fire the one who has the lower Profit number). If both people were getting their Profit % from Essbase, then they'd at least have the same number. While this doesn't guarantee that Essbase was calculating it correctly, at least everyone was using the same incorrect number.

The other nice benefit of performing the calculation in Essbase is that the next time you need the calculation. You don't have to remember how you calculated it last time. There's a member waiting for you to use with the calculation already defined. Sample.Basic, for instance, has members called "Profit %" and "Margin %" in the Measures dimension. Go ahead and type Profit % into cell A18 and *Refresh*. You'll see that Profit as a percent of Sales is about 26% for the year.

While adding all of your calculations to Essbase may be great in theory, there are plenty of times when a calculation will occur to you on the spot and you don't want to bother your Essbase admin, asking her to add the calculation to the database. For instance, say we want to add a line to our report that calculates Total Expenses as a percent of Sales. "Expense %" is not a member in the database. Type in the following:

- In cell A20, "Expense %"
- In cell B20, "=B15/B9*100"

Copy the formula in cell B20 to cells C20:E20. Your report should now look like this:

	A	B	C	D	E
1		Profit and Loss Analysis			
2					
3		Market:	Market		
4		Product:	Product		
5		Scenario:	Actual		
6					
7					
8		Qtr1	Qtr2	Qtr3	Qtr4
9	Sales	95820	101679	105215	98141
10	COGS	42877	45362	47343	43754
11	Margin	52943	56317	57872	54387
12	Marketing	15839	16716	17522	16160
13	Payroll	12168	12243	12168	12168
14	Misc	233	251	270	259
15	Total Expenses	28240	29210	29960	28587
16	Profit	24703	27107	27912	25800
17					
18	Profit %	25.78063	26.65939	26.52854	26.28871
19					
20	Expense %	29.47193	28.72766	28.47503	29.1285

Formulas can be in the rows or the columns just like a normal Excel spreadsheet. Refresh your data and something really cool will happen: your Expense % formulas remains.

By default, Smart View will retain formulas. In the old days of the Excel Add-in, we had to turn on Formula Note! Preservation.

Save your report. Now drill into Qtr1 and see what happens?

Not so disastrous: just a few updates required. Now try moving Product to the rows. See what we mean about making sure your layout is final? Don't save this mess and let's get back to step 6.

Note!

If you use Smart View for Planning, FM or Enterprise you may see an option *Preserve Formula on POV Change*. Unfortunately, this option is not available for Essbase connections.

Step 6: Apply Formatting

Once you get to step 6, Essbase's work is done and it's up to you, Excel Jockey. Format to your heart's content: just don't forget to check the *Use Excel Formatting* option first.

Try It!

Take your existing report and apply whatever Excel formatting you want.

Here's our early report with some centering, borders, underlining, bolding, and number formatting (and the gridlines turned off):

	A	B	C	D	E
1		Profit and Loss Analysis			
2					
3		*Market:*	Market		
4		*Product:*	Product		
5		*Scenario:*	Actual		
6					
7					
8		Qtr1	Qtr2	Qtr3	Qtr4
9	Sales	$ 95,820	$ 101,679	$ 105,215	$ 98,141
10	COGS	$ 42,877	$ 45,362	$ 47,343	$ 43,754
11	*Margin*	*$ 52,943*	*$ 56,317*	*$ 57,872*	*$ 54,387*
12	Marketing	$ 15,839	$ 16,716	$ 17,522	$ 16,160
13	Payroll	$ 12,168	$ 12,243	$ 12,168	$ 12,168
14	Misc	$ 233	$ 251	$ 270	$ 259
15	*Total Expenses*	*$ 28,240*	*$ 29,210*	*$ 29,960*	*$ 28,587*
16	Profit	$ 24,703	$ 27,107	$ 27,912	$ 25,800
17					
18	Profit %	26	27	27	26
19					
20	Expense %	29	29	28	29
21					

Step 7: Save

Before you save the workbook, blank out all your numbers (keep your formulas, though). This makes the file size that much smaller thereby making the file that much faster to open next time.

The next time you want to use this report, open it up, connect to the database, use Member Select to select your Market, Product, and Scenario members (or just type them in), and finally choose *Refresh*.

Save your spreadsheet where you'll be able to find it later. We'll be using it in future exercises.

Try It!

CELL STYLE OPTIONS

We've already reviewed the most common and, in our opinion, best formatting option in Smart View but we must cover two other options available to you: Cell Styles and Capture Data Formatting. Cell Styles will apply specific formatting (fonts, borders, and backgrounds to member and data cells). Formatting can be assigned by different characteristics of members and data cells. You may also want to highlight a specific member or data points for a particular reason. For example, we recommend using cell styles for members or data points that may have drill through reports associated with them. If you are inputting data, you may want to apply a special format to highlight intersections with write access.

To use cell Styles. Select *Hyperion >> Options* or click the *Options* button. Select the *Styles* tab:

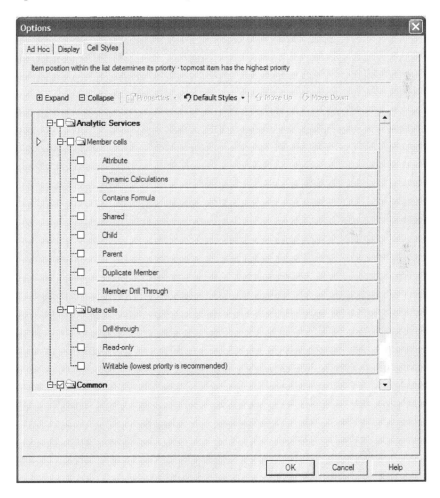

Before we start, make a copy of the formatted P&L report. Remove the "page" selections for Market, Product, and Scenario so that those dimensions will be added back to the POV. Next select the Display tab and uncheck the *Use Excel Formatting* checkbox. In order to use cell styles, Excel formatting must be turned off. (So you will have to weigh which option you will use.)

Next select the *Cell Styles* tab and expand the *Analytic Services* option. Expand *Member cells* to set member properties or expand *Data cells* to set data cell properties:

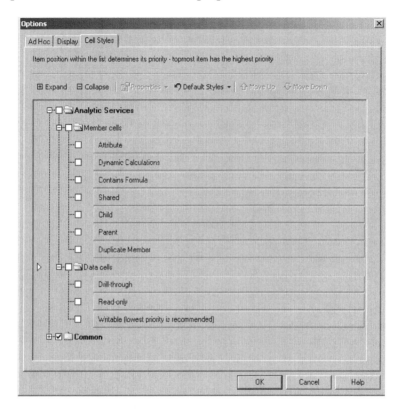

 Note! What's Analytic Services? Back in the old days just as System 9 was introduced and when Hyperion still owned Hyperion, Essbase was renamed to Analytic Services. Thank goodness for Oracle as they have now brought home our beloved Essbase name back to us. Still you may see references to "Analytic Services" throughout the Oracle EPM products. Just think "Essbase" when you see this.

Let's change the cell style for parents. Check the box next to *Parent* to enable a properties box:

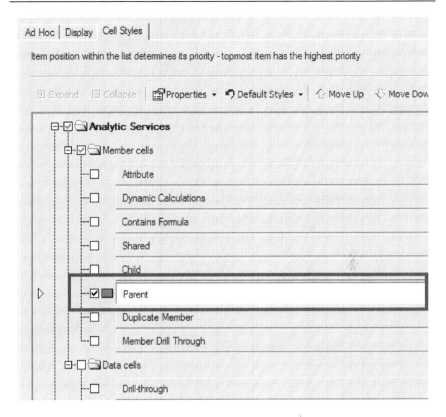

You can set the properties for *Font*, *Background*, and *Border*. From the Properties drop down, choose *Font*:

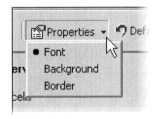

Change the font to bold and some nice earth tone (navy is the new black):

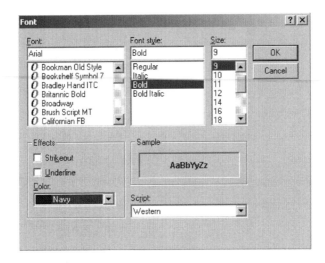

Click *OK* and then click *OK* again to save the settings and close the Options window. Refresh data.

Here is the result:

	A	B	C	D	E
1		Qtr1	Qtr2	Qtr3	Qtr4
2	Sales	95820	101679	105215	98141
3	COGS	42877	45362	47343	43754
4	Margin	52943	56317	57872	54387
5	Marketing	15839	16716	17522	16160
6	Payroll	12168	12243	12168	12168
7	Misc	233	251	270	259
8	Total Expenses	28240	29210	29960	28587
9	Profit	24703	27107	27912	25800
10					

Notice for any member that is a parent, the font is now bold and a nice earthy "navy" tone. Any member that is a child only (level-zero) is set to the default formatting. If you wanted all members to have the same formatting, go back to the *Options >> Cell Styles* tab and set the same font properties for the Child section.

A member can meet more than one criterion. Qtr1 is both a parent and a child. Yo Mamma is both a parent (yours) and a child (of yo Grandmamma). Use the *Move Up* or *Move Down* buttons to define the order of precedence for how cell styles should be applied:

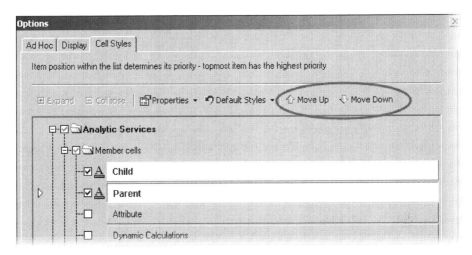

The cells at the top of the list have higher precedence while cells at the bottom of the list have lower precedence.

On Data cells, you can set a background color for writable cells (along with font or border settings). Setting a background color is beneficial when developing budgeting input sheets for end user submissions. In the example below, read-only cells are set to gray and writable cells are set to yellow:

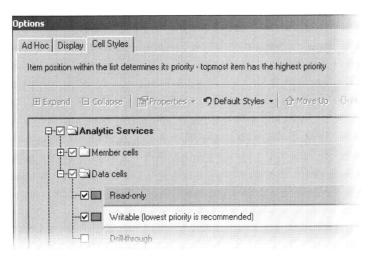

Here is an example of a budget entry spreadsheet with Cell Styles applied:

	A	B	C	D	E	
1			Jan	Feb	Mar	
2			Budget	Budget	Budget	
3	New York	Sales	640	610	640	
4	Massachusetts	Sales	460	440	460	
5	Florida	Sales	190	190	190	
6	Connecticut	Sales	290	300	290	
7	New Hampshire	Sales	110	100	110	
8	East	Sales	1690	1640	1690	
9						
10						

Tip!

You may want to also set Dynamically calc'd cells to grey so that you know you can't load data to that member (remember our earlier discussion on dynamically calculated members?).

Try It!

Create your own budget entry spreadsheet for Sample.Basic. Show it to all your friends. See if you still have friends afterwards.

Note!

Make sure you uncheck *Use Excel Formatting* on the *Display* tab. If this option is selected, Cell Styles are ignored.

Once you're finished playing with Styles (and before burning matching holes in your retinas due to horrendous color schemes), go to the *Styles* tab on your Options and uncheck all the boxes on the *Style* tab.

Note!

Turning off Styles does not set your spreadsheet back to its "pre-Essbase" formatting. You may have to click *Refresh* or set Excel formatting to return the desired state.

CAPTURE FORMATTING OF DATA CELLS

The last formatting feature available in Smart View is the ability to save the formatting defined for data cells. This feature is more helpful as you perform adhoc analysis vs. creating formatted reports. Open a blank worksheet and retrieve data for

Sample.Basic. Zoom in on Year. Set the formatting for the data cells to $ using Excel formatting:

	A	B
1		Measures
2	Qtr1	$ 24,703.00
3	Qtr2	$ 27,107.00
4	Qtr3	$ 27,912.00
5	Qtr4	$ 25,800.00
6	Year	$ 105,522.00

Make sure *Use Excel Formatting* under *Options* is still unchecked. Next, select the data cells with the formatting defined (just the data cells). Select *Hyperion >> Adhoc Analysis >> Capture Formatting*:

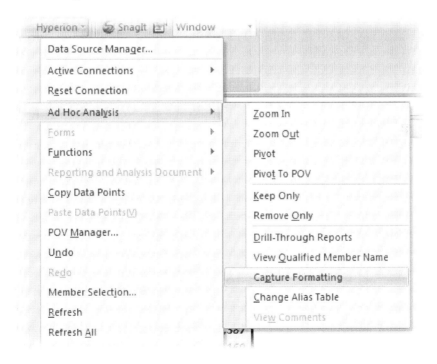

Now when you perform a refresh or basic drilling, the cell formatting will remain for the selected cells. Zoom into Qtr1 and you should see the following ($ for the quarters and no formatting for Jan, Feb, and Mar):

	A	B
1		Measures
2	Jan	8024
3	Feb	8346
4	Mar	8333
5	Qtr1	$ 24,703.00
6	Qtr2	$ 27,107.00
7	Qtr3	$ 27,912.00
8	Qtr4	$ 25,800.00
9	Year	$ 105,522.00

Note! Captured formatting is tied to specific member combinations. If you drill down, next levels will not have the applied formatting.

The other alternative in analysis is to check *Use Excel Formatting* and *Retain Numeric Formatting* which will keep the number formatting as you perform analysis. The benefit is that it applies the same numeric formatting as you drill into dimensions or change the layout. It won't however keep other types of formatting like borders, colors, and fonts.

	Capture Formatting	*Retain Numeric Formatting*
Applies to Data Cells	Y	Y
Applies to Members	N	N
Numeric Formatting Only	N	Y
Retains numeric formatting on drill	Y - for specific cells only	Y – format fills for all cells
Retains formatting on POV change	Y- for specific cells only	Y
Retains formatting on pivot	Y - for specific cells only	Y

So which option should I use when creating formatted reports? In most cases, we recommend using Excel Formatting for your highly formatted reports (following our 7 step approach). The following chart provides a quick comparison of the formatting features:

	Capture Formatting	*Use Excel Formatting*
Applies to Data Cells	Y	Y
Applies to Members	N	Y
Retains formatting on drill	Y (for specific cells)	N
Retains formatting on POV change	Y	Y
Retains formatting on pivot	Y (for specific cells)	N

Now that Lumbergh is happy with your nicely formatted reports, he's asked you to create the same version of the P&L report for each different product (and you have over 1000 products). Before you start thinking "I'm just not gonna go" again, let us introduce you to our friend, the magician known as Cascade (you click a button and reports magically appear).

CASCADE

Once you start building reports, the time will come when you want to run the same report for multiple selections. On the report you just built, you might want to run it for every region. While you could use Member Select to pick each region (East, Central...) and choose *Refresh* after each one, there a new feature in version 11 called Cascade that allows do this in a much faster manner.

For our example, we've been asked to create a P&L by product. Open our saved P&L report and connect to Sample.Basic:

	A	B	C	D	E
1		Profit and Loss Analysis			
2					
3		*Market:*	Market		
4		*Product:*	Product		
5		*Scenario:*	Actual		
6					
7					
8		Qtr1	Qtr2	Qtr3	Qtr4
9	Sales	$ 95,820	$ 101,679	$ 105,215	$ 98,141
10	COGS	$ 42,877	$ 45,362	$ 47,343	$ 43,754
11	*Margin*	*$ 52,943*	*$ 56,317*	*$ 57,872*	*$ 54,387*
12	Marketing	$ 15,839	$ 16,716	$ 17,522	$ 16,160
13	Payroll	$ 12,168	$ 12,243	$ 12,168	$ 12,168
14	Misc	$ 233	$ 251	$ 270	$ 259
15	*Total Expenses*	*$ 28,240*	*$ 29,210*	*$ 29,960*	*$ 28,587*
16	Profit	$ 24,703	$ 27,107	$ 27,912	$ 25,800
17					
18	Profit %	26	27	27	26
19					
20	Expense %	29	29	28	29
21					

Click the *Cascade Adhoc Grid* icon in the Data Source Manager window:

If you are using our example, you received the following error message:

The dimension for which you are cascading (or bursting) must be in the POV. Simply select cells B4 and C4 and hit delete (if you drag the Product dimension to the POV window, you will lose all of your formatting). Click *Refresh.*

Now click the *Cascade* icon. Using the Member Selection, choose children of Product (a.k.a Product Category):

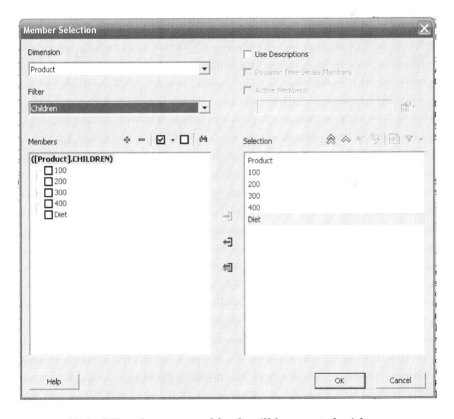

Click *OK* and a new workbook will be created with a worksheet for each product category:

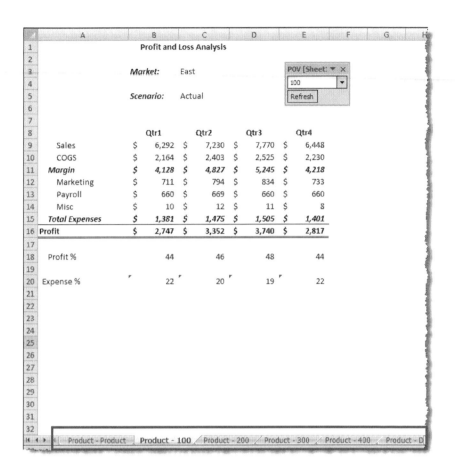

You may be directed back to the original spreadsheet but never fear, the new workbook is there. Was it really that easy to generate reports for all of my product categories? Yes, it was: imagine the possibilities. We now have a number of reports created in a just a few seconds. Imagine running this for hundreds of stores. Go have a venti latte with the time we've just saved you.

Note!

The tabs in the cascaded workbook are renamed to either the member name or alias depending on what you have selected for the current connection. (Remember in the old days when the Excel Add-in just numbered the spreadsheets. Yes, my old friend the Excel Add-in, we think it is about time you retired.)

MULTI-SOURCE REPORTS

There are certain times when you'll want to have two sets of Essbase data on one sheet. Say we wanted to create a report that had Actual on the top half of the page and Budget on the bottom half:

		Qtr1	Market Qtr2	Product Qtr3	Actual Qtr4	Year
	Sales	95,820	101,679	105,215	98,141	**400,855**
	COGS	42,877	45,362	47,343	43,754	**179,336**
	Margin	52,943	56,317	57,872	54,387	**221,519**
	Marketing	15,839	16,716	17,522	16,160	**66,237**
	Payroll	12,168	12,243	12,168	12,168	**48,747**
	Misc	233	251	270	259	**1,013**
	Total Expenses	28,240	29,210	29,960	28,587	**115,997**
	Profit	**24,703**	**27,107**	**27,912**	**25,800**	**105,522**
		Qtr1	Market Qtr2	Product Qtr3	Budget Qtr4	Year
	Sales	89,680	95,240	98,690	89,470	**373,080**
	COGS	38,140	40,460	42,280	38,060	**158,940**
	Margin	51,540	54,780	56,410	51,410	**214,140**
	Marketing	11,900	12,700	13,370	11,550	**49,520**
	Payroll	9,060	9,210	9,060	7,910	**35,240**
	Misc	-	-	-	-	**-**
	Total Expenses	20,960	21,910	22,430	19,460	**84,760**
	Profit	**30,580**	**32,870**	**33,980**	**31,950**	**129,380**

In the old Excel Add-in, if you created this spreadsheet and chose *Essbase >> Retrieve*, you'd receive the following error:

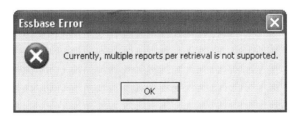

This was actually our favorite Essbase Add-In error, because it almost comes across as a poorly worded marketing message. The presence of the word "Currently" gives you hope that if you just wait until the next release, Essbase will support multiple reports per retrieval! Not to dash your hopes, but this error message has been there for over ten years and they still haven't added it. Give up and stop waiting, because there is a workaround (check out our *Look Smarter Than You Are with Essbase System 9: An End User's Guide* for those steps).

So is it possible in Smart View? Of course, using our new friends, the data points. Let's use the following example: we need to combine data from our US database (a.k.a. Sample.Basic) and our international database (a.k.a. Sample.Interntl) into one report. On one worksheet, create the following query for Sample.Basic:

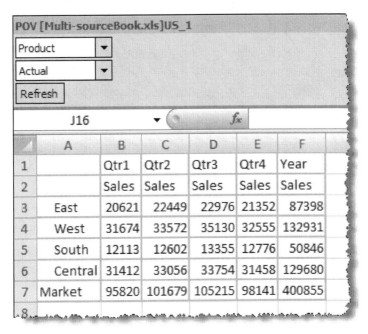

On a second worksheet, create the following query for Sample.Interntl:

POV [Multi-sourceBook.xls]Interntl_1					
Product ▼					
Actual ▼					
Refresh					

B17	▼			f_x	
	A	B	C	D	E	F
1		Qtr1	Qtr2	Qtr3	Qtr4	Year
2		Sales	Sales	Sales	Sales	Sales
3	US	95820	101679	105215	98141	400855
4	Canada	16461.27	16505.64	16781.04	16351.11	66099.06
5	Europe	21335.923	26254.93	28680.47	24925.64	101196.963
6	Market	133617.193	144439.57	150676.51	139417.75	568151.023

Next, select the first grid from the worksheet and select *Copy* from the Hyperion ribbon. Using the Smart View *Paste* button in the Hyperion ribbon, paste the data points into a blank worksheet. Repeat the same steps for the second grid, copying and pasting the data points below the first grid. Notice each data cell is an individual data point that is tied to a specific intersection of dimension members, database and server. Click *Refresh* to refresh the data for each data point:

E4	▼		f_x	= HsGetValue("", "Year#Qtr4",
	A	B	C	D	E	F
1						
2	◇	Qtr1	Qtr2	Qtr3	Qtr4	Year
3		Sales	Sales	Sales	Sales	Sales
4	US	95820	101679	105215	98141	400855
5	Canada	16461.27	16505.64	16781.04	16351.11	66099.06
6	Europe	21335.92	26254.93	28680.47	24925.64	101197
7	Market	133617.2	144439.6	150676.5	139417.8	568151
8						
9						
10		Qtr1	Qtr2	Qtr3	Qtr4	Year
11		Sales	Sales	Sales	Sales	Sales
12	East	20621	22449	22976	21352	87398
13	West	31674	33572	35130	32555	132931
14	South	12113	12602	13355	12776	50846
15	Central	31412	33056	33754	31458	129680
16	Market	95820	101679	105215	98141	400855
17						

From this point you can follow the same 7 steps to a formatted report. You can then refresh the report daily, monthly or as necessary and the current data stored in Essbase will display.

Notice that if you select the data point a tool tip will display showing you the attributes about the data point. Notice all of our data points reference Product. What if we wanted to run this report for product category for 200? How do I change each cell and more importantly, is there a way to change it once for all data points?

We'll show you how you can do this once for each data source. Select a data point in our multi-source report and choose *POV Manager*. The POV Manager will display showing the two main Smart View queries used for the data points:

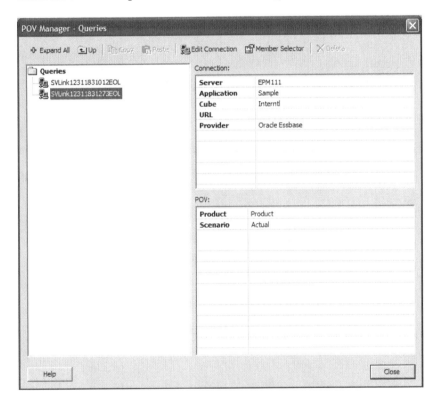

For each SVLinkxxx (one for Sample.Basic and one for Sample.Interntl), change the Product dimension selection from Product to 200 by highlighting the product and using the Member selection window:

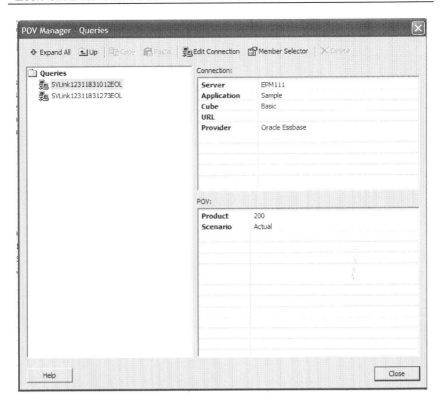

Click *Close*. Choose *Refresh* and note all of the data points are updated for the product category 200.

CREATE A REPORT IN WORD OR POWERPOINT

As we mentioned earlier Smart View works with Excel as well as Word and PowerPoint. Integration with all of the Office products are bread and butter for Smart View. The easiest way to get data into Word or PowerPoint is by copying and pasting data points just as we did in the Power User chapter. You can copy and paste data points from:

- Excel to Word and PowerPoint
- Word to Word and PowerPoint
- PowerPoint to Word and PowerPoint

These live data points are tied to a specific server, database and dimension member intersection (just like the data points in Excel). This means you can refresh them at any time and get the most current data.

When creating reports in Word or PowerPoint, make sure to apply Excel formatting first before you copy and paste data points to Word and PowerPoint. The numeric formatting is preserved as you copy and paste the data points. Member formatting however is not saved. You'll need to apply desired formatting in Word or PowerPoint.

Let's now create another report in Word. Pull up our saved formatted report. Note in our example we've chosen the East market, Diet products, and the Actual scenario. Select the grid portion of the report and choose *Copy Data* from the Hyperion ribbon:

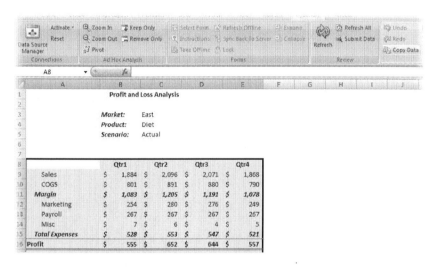

Next open a blank Word document. Add a title and text to the word document (just to give you a feel for what is possible):

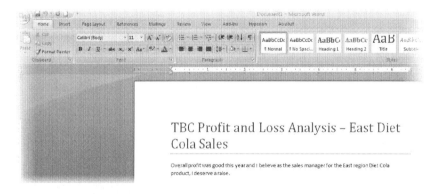

Find the desired location for the copied grid and choose *Paste Data* from the Hyperion ribbon and the result should look as follows:

TBC Profit and Loss Analysis – East Diet Cola Sales

Overall profit was good this year and I believe as the sales manager for the East region Diet Cola product, I deserve a raise.

	Qtr1	Qtr2	Qtr3	Qtr4
Sales	#NEED_REFRESH	#NEED_REFRESH	#NEED_REFRESH	#NEED_REFRESH
COGS	#NEED_REFRESH	#NEED_REFRESH	#NEED_REFRESH	#NEED_REFRESH
Margin	#NEED_REFRESH	#NEED_REFRESH	#NEED_REFRESH	#NEED_REFRESH
Marketing	#NEED_REFRESH	#NEED_REFRESH	#NEED_REFRESH	#NEED_REFRESH
Payroll	#NEED_REFRESH	#NEED_REFRESH	#NEED_REFRESH	#NEED_REFRESH
Misc	#NEED_REFRESH	#NEED_REFRESH	#NEED_REFRESH	#NEED_REFRESH
Total Expenses	#NEED_REFRESH	#NEED_REFRESH	#NEED_REFRESH	#NEED_REFRESH
Profit	#NEED_REFRESH	#NEED_REFRESH	#NEED_REFRESH	#NEED_REFRESH

Click *Refresh* to retrieve the data. Apply some formatting using Word and the result should look as follows:

TBC Profit and Loss Analysis – East Diet Cola Sales

Overall profit was good this year and I believe as the sales manager for the East region Diet Cola product, I deserve a raise.

	Qtr1	Qtr2	Qtr3	Qtr4
Sales	$ 1,884	$ 2,096	$ 2,071	$ 1,868
COGS	$ 801	$ 891	$ 880	$ 790
Margin	*$ 1,083*	*$ 1,205*	*$ 1,191*	*$ 1,078*
Marketing	$ 254	$ 280	$ 276	$ 249
Payroll	$ 267	$ 267	$ 267	$ 267
Misc	$ 7	$ 6	$ 4	$ 5
Total Expenses	*$ 528*	*$ 553*	*$ 547*	*$ 521*
Profit	**$ 555**	**$ 652**	**$ 644**	**$ 557**

As the underlying data changes, you can simply click *Refresh* to pull in the current data set. In this basic example, we've shown you how to pull in data from a single source but you can create multi-source reports in Word and PowerPoint as well.

You can change the POV for the data points just as we did in Excel. Choose sales for Qtr3 and select *POV Manager*. Change the Market member selection to Market and Product member selection to Product:

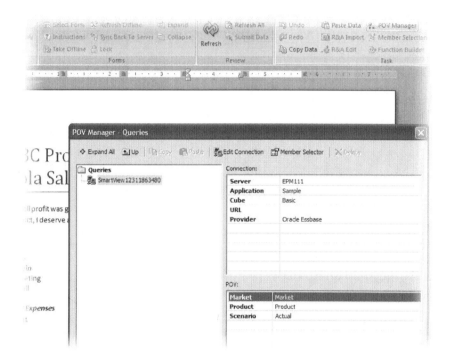

Click *Close* to close the POV Manager and click *Refresh*. The data points in the report should be updated to reflect the new member selections.

Follow these same steps to create a presentation in PowerPoint and don't forget the ability to *Visualize in Excel* (amaze your boss with immediate answers during presentation reviews).

Tip!

To Visualize in Excel, you must select a specific data point (not the table).

Now you can see the reporting options are practically endless with Smart View and our hand Office products. But we're not done yet! Hold on as we jump into two big new features introduced in Smart View 11, Smart Slices and Report Designer.

Chapter 6:
Smart Slices & Report Designer

By now you may be asking yourself, what more could I need with Essbase and my trusty Smart View add-in. We just covered how to create reports and report templates with our Essbase database and that was pretty easy. Can it get any better? See for yourself as we review the new 11.1 features called Smart Slices and Report Designer. Read closely as the topics we cover here could prove beneficial for your upcoming presentation with Lumbergh, the consultants and executive management.

SMART SLICES

Introduction to Smart Slices

Smart Slices, introduced in version 11, allow an administrator or interactive user to create a filtered data view for a selected cube. For the DBAs reading this book, smart slices are like a view against an Essbase database. For example, you have a Sales Analysis database for all markets across the United States. However, the Sales Managers only care about analyzing data for their specific region (o.k., you're right, they probably want to sneak a peek at their performance in comparison to the other markets but let's roll with this example anyway). You can create a smart slice for each market, filtering the dimensions and data and setting up a starting point query for the end users. This saves the user time in navigating through the hierarchy to find their "market". They are immediately ready to start analyzing. Users can further filter the smart slice using a sub-query (more on this in a bit). Defining and using smart slices is also another way of distributing and sharing a default point of view for a data source. Once the smart slice is defined, the users can perform analysis and create reports just as they do with a regular Essbase connection (e.g. zoom in, pivot, member select).

Smart slices are only available in Smart View (not visible to the Workspace...today; this functionality will be coming in future versions). So for what products can you create smart slices? Essbase, OBIEE, and Planning sources. We are of course focusing on Essbase in this book but the steps for defining and using smart slices are similar across the above mentioned sources.

Create a Smart Slice

The best way to understand smart slices is to create and actually use one so let's get started.

Only administrators and interactive users can create smart slices. If you don't see the *Add* option in your right click menu, give your administrator a call and make your case for why you need to create smart slices or ask her to create the sample Smart Slice below for you. In the meantime, jump down to the *Use a Smart Slice* section and follow along in your mind.

Note!

The Smart Slice requires the Common Provider Service (APS). Essentially you must be using version 11 and the common connections for Smart View (you can't use an Independent connection to create a Smart Slice).

In a blank sheet, connect to Sample.Basic. Right click on the Sample.Basic database and click *Add*:

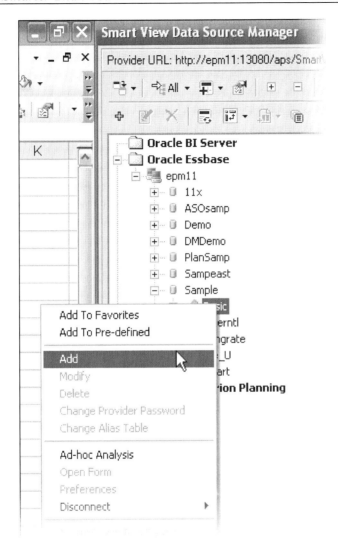

You will be prompted to select an alias table. Choose *Default* and click *OK:*

The default Smart Slice definition will display. Note the default is descendants of every dimension (the entire cube):

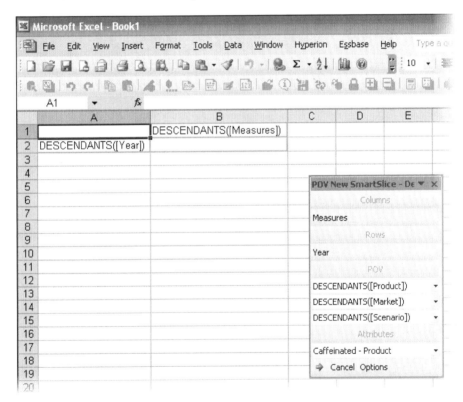

Using member selection and drag/dropping capabilities (similar to the Query Designer), update the Smart Slice definition to select the descendants of West and Sales.

Double click on Measures in the POV New SmartSlice Definition window. Change the member filter (if necessary) to Descendants. Note that if the filter is set to Children, you only see the children of Measures. Select *Sales* and use the right arrow button to move Sales into the Selection section.

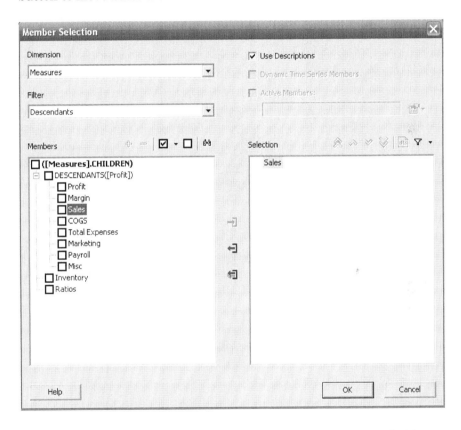

From the drop down box on the POV Smart Slice Definition window, select the ellipses (...) for Market:

Remove the selection for the descendants of Market by clicking the double left arrow icon. Select *West* and use the arrow icon to move West into the Selection section. Click the Filter icon in the mid-level right hand portion of the Member Selection window and choose Descendants:

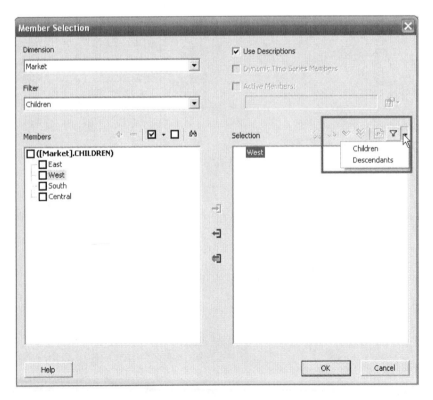

The result should look like the following:

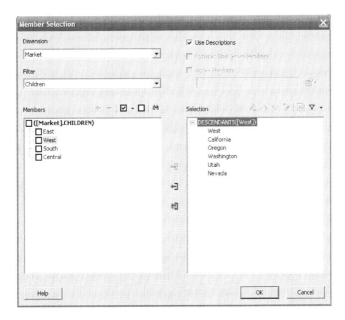

Click *OK* and your smart slice definition and spreadsheet should now look like this:

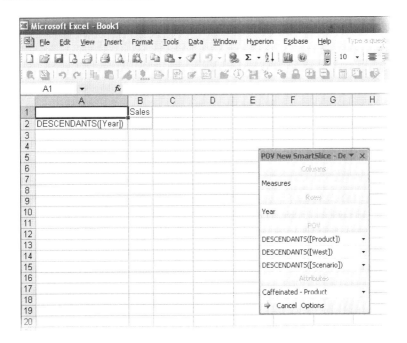

You can define options for smart slices like indentions or display for missing data. Click *Options* on the POV New SmartSlice Definition window to define the preferences for the Smart Slice. In this example, let us set the following options:

- Replace #Missing label with a -.
- Set Thousands separator to *Yes*.
- Confirm the Alias table is set to *Default*.

Click *OK* when the options are set. Next, drag Descendants(West) to the Rows. Drag Scenario to the Column. Move Measures and Years to the POV (you could have also moved these dimensions the start of the process):

Click the *Green Arrow (Done)* button when the Smart Slice Definition is complete:

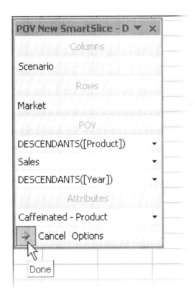

At this point (in our example), we will be prompted to specify members for the POV (Product, Sales and Year).

The default values are the top members for Product and Year and our only option for Measures – Sales. We can leave the defaults or use Member Selection to change the selections, further filtering the smart slice:

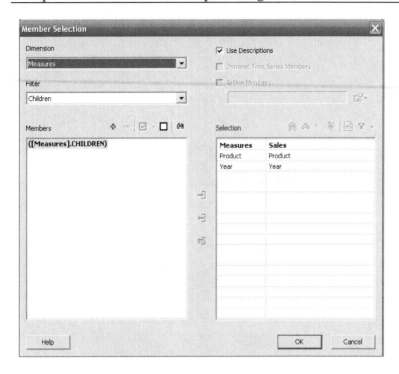

For now leave the selected members and click *OK*. Enter a new name for the Smart Slice – *WestSales*:

Click the revolving green arrows to accept the new name:

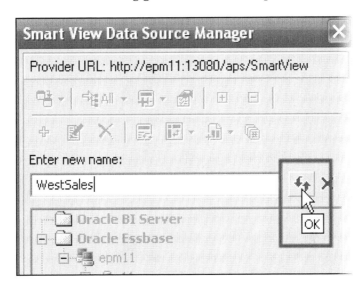

The new slice is added to the Sample.Basic database, indicated by the pink cube under the blue Basic cube.

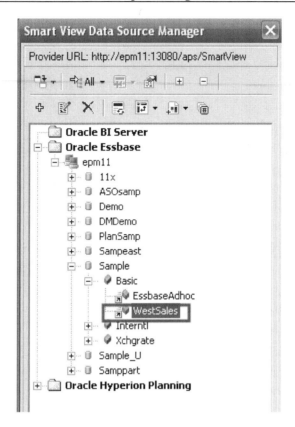

Note that you can have multiple smart slices for a single Essbase database. But beware and don't create so many smart slices that it becomes difficult to use and manage. In version 11.1.1.1 there is not a way to assign or security these smart slices by user or group. Everyone sees every smart slice. There isn't a way to organize the smart slices either so you may want to think through the naming conventions for the smart slices ahead of time (smart slices are sorted alphabetically).

Note!

Even thought Smart Slices are not secured by user, Essbase assigned member and data security still apply.

Use a Smart Slice

To analyze data with smart slices, simply right click on the WestSales Smart Slice and click *Ad-hoc Analysis*:

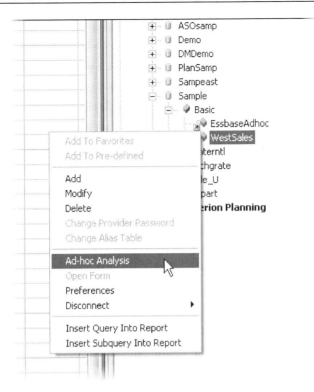

You may be prompted with this message depending on if you are in a blank spreadsheet or spreadsheet with data. We've seen this before but as a reminder, if you need to save the data in the current spreadsheet, click *No*. To replace the data in the current spreadsheet with the default view for the Smart Slice click *Yes*.

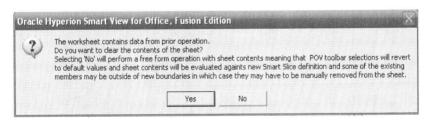

The following result should display:

You are immediately brought into the default layout and definition of the smart slice, with West in my rows, Scenario in the column and a focus on sales. We don't see data because we didn't specify Scenario. Double click on Scenario to view Actual, Budget and Variance information.

Zoom into West. Zoom back up and notice that you can't go any higher then West. When using the smart slice you are limited to the selections for the smart slice. Pivot Product to the rows and drill down on product, noting you have full analytical functionality within the smart slice.

Hmm… maybe we should have designed the smart slice to automatically display Actual, Budget and Variance. Can I modify my smart slice? Of course.

Modify a Smart Slice

To modify a smart slice, simply right click and select *Edit>>Modify*. Let's do that now for our WestSales smart slice. When the smart slice definition window displays, double click on Scenario. In the Member Selection window, update the selection to specifically select Actual, Budget, Variance, and Var %.

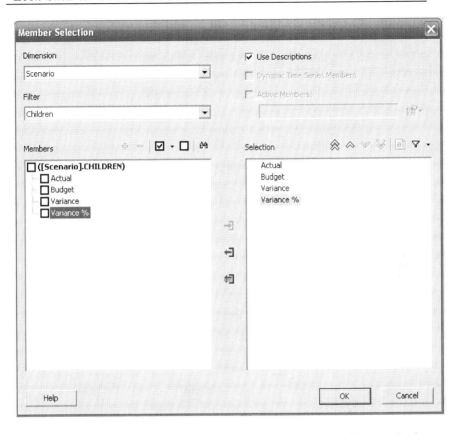

Click *OK* and your smart slice definition should now look like the following:

Click the *Green Arrow* icon to save your changes and click *OK* at the member selection screen to accept the default members selected. The following result should display:

Try It!

Create another smart slice similar to your West Sales smart slice but this time for East Sales.

Note!

If someone else is maintaining your Smart Slices for you, select the Sync with Smart slices icon to sync up your view with the current Smart Slice definition.

Now that we know how to create and use smart slices, let's learn about Report Designer.

REPORT DESIGNER

Introduction to Report Designer

In addition to Smart Slices, version 11 introduces (drum roll, please) a new user interface that uses existing Smart Slices to create formatted and structured reports. But we've already created nice, formatted reports? Think what've we've done so far on steroids. That's the Report Designer. The Report Designer leverages Office – Excel, Word or PowerPoint – for report design. You can combine multiple grids into a document and link controls for those grids. Those sources that leverage the common provider services can take advantage of the Report Designer.

Note!

Quiz: What sources in version 11.1.1.1 use the common provider Services? Essbase, Planning, and OBI Server. A+ for you!

Without further ado, let's create a report in Report Designer so that you can fully understand the power of this new tool (imagine the evil laugh of Diego DeSilva as Dr. Dementor ... ah ha ha ha).

Note!

Any Smart View user can use smart slices and create reports with Report Designer (not limited to administrators and interactive users).

Create a Report with Report Designer

In a blank worksheet, create the following report title and heading:

	A	B	C	D
1	**Product Sales Report**			
2				
3	East Region			
4				
5				

Next add the Smart Slice to the Report Designer by clicking on the East Sales smart slice and selecting *Insert into Query into Report*:

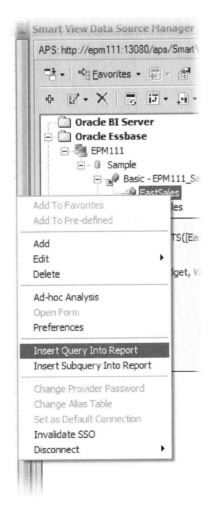

The Smart Slice should be added to the Report Designer (this is called a query). The Report Designer is the section under the server and applications listing within the Data Source Manager. Right click on the "query" and note the available options. Skipping the Query View / Dimensional View options (we'll cover those in just a moment), see that we have three types of data objects: Function Grid, Table, and Chart and two control objects: Slider and POV.

Object	Description
Function Grid	Displays the query in a dynamic grid format; Data points are inserted into individual cells in Excel, individual data points in a Word table, and individual data points in PowerPoint text boxes
Table	Displays results in a grid format that floats on the document and can be moved and resized. Scroll bars within the table allow you to view larger sets of data in smaller spaces.
Chart	Displays results in a chart format that floats on the document and can be moved and resized.
Slider Control	Control based on one dimension and the defined set of members. Users "slide" the selection to choose different members.
POV Control	Control based on multiple dimensions (those not used in the query in the rows or columns). Users select members from the POV using Member Selection.

Let's see these objects in action. Select insert a *Function Grid*:

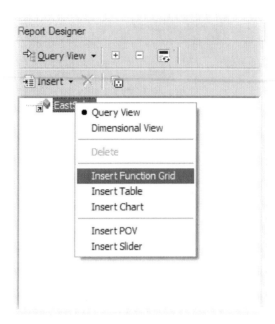

The EastSales Smart Slice should be inserted into the spreadsheet as follows:

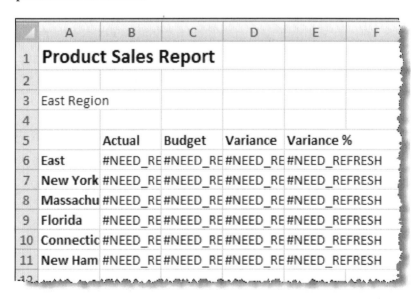

	A	B	C	D	E	F
1	**Product Sales Report**					
2						
3	East Region					
4						
5		**Actual**	**Budget**	**Variance**	**Variance %**	
6	**East**	#NEED_RE	#NEED_RE	#NEED_RE	#NEED_REFRESH	
7	**New York**	#NEED_RE	#NEED_RE	#NEED_RE	#NEED_REFRESH	
8	**Massachu**	#NEED_RE	#NEED_RE	#NEED_RE	#NEED_REFRESH	
9	**Florida**	#NEED_RE	#NEED_RE	#NEED_RE	#NEED_REFRESH	
10	**Connectic**	#NEED_RE	#NEED_RE	#NEED_RE	#NEED_REFRESH	
11	**New Ham**	#NEED_RE	#NEED_RE	#NEED_RE	#NEED_REFRESH	

Click *Refresh* and the data will display. When you refresh a function grid, the data cells are refreshed and members are not. This would be a problem if let's say you created a report with a list of products in the rows. If a new product is added to the database, the report will not dynamically refresh, adding in the new product. If you need to refresh both the data and members (as in our product listing example), you must re-insert the function grid. You could also consider using a table instead (more on tables in just a moment).

Tip!

To apply formatting to function grids, simply use Excel formatting. Formatting defined in the Smart Slice options will not flow through and display in Report Designer objects.

Tip!

Another cool feature is that you can use Excel formulas with function grids. You must leave one empty row between the grid and the cell containing the formula and include the empty row in the range of cells selected for the formula definition.

Next select cell A14 and right click on EastSales "query" in the Report Designer and select *Insert Chart*:

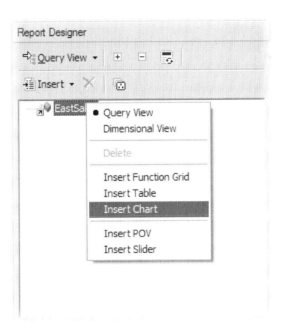

The chart will be inserted into the spreadsheet. Resize and move the chart as desired:

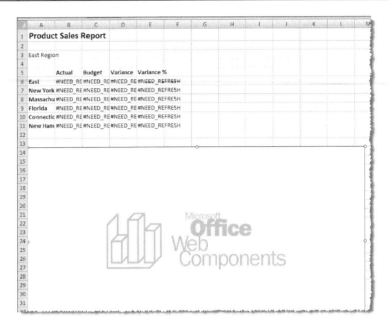

Select *Refresh* (or choose *Hyperion >> Refresh*) and the report is populated with the Essbase data:

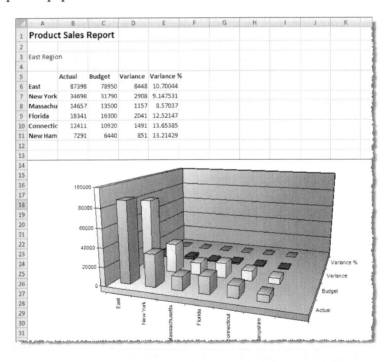

Select cell A40. Right click on East Sales query and select *Insert >> Table*. Resize the table accordingly:

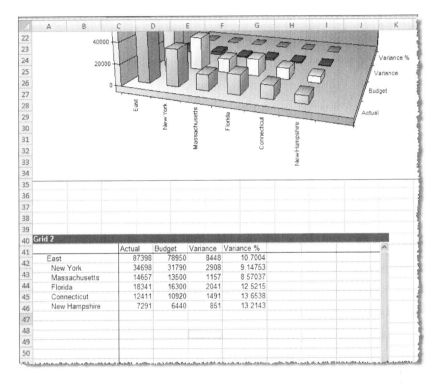

After the initial positioning, you must be in Excel Developer mode to resize or move the charts or tables.

Tip!

To enable the Excel Developer mode, select the Office icon in the upper left corner of the screen. Choose the *Excel Options* button. Check the *Show Developer tab in the Ribbon* option:

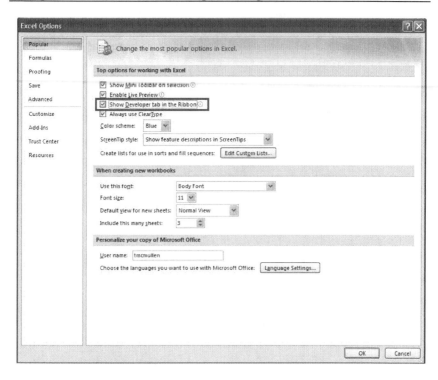

The Developer tab should display. Select *Design Mode* and resize the objects accordingly:

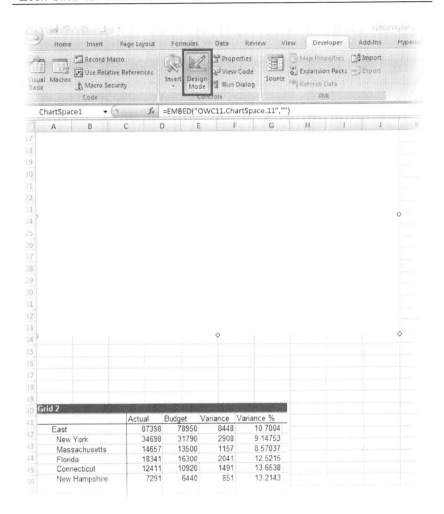

As we mentioned earlier, the table is a floating grid object that contains linked members and data. If you perform a refresh, both members and data will be re-queried and displayed to the user (whereas function grids only refresh the data).

In our example, double click on East and notice that you can zoom in and out within a table. However, other analytic adhoc features are not available against tables.

Let's review the use cases for function grids versus tables:

Why Function Grids?

- Function grids are most useful for reports in which members remain reasonably static
- Member formulas / formula preservation

- Data point inserted into a cell
- Available in Excel, Word, PowerPoint

Why Tables?
- For reports whose members that change often (tables will refresh both the members and the data)
- Basic zooming
- Show large amount of data in smaller display areas
- Available in Excel, PowerPoint

Now that we've inserted the content of the report, let's use some controls to select the members for the remaining dimensions. We'll start with the slider control. The slider displays a selected set of dimension members from a query. When you drag the slider marker to a member, its data is displayed in all reports associated with the query on the sheet.

Go back to the top of the report and insert several rows just below the report title:

	A	B	C	D	E	F
1	**Product Sales Report**					
2						
3						
4						
5						
6	East Region					
7						
8		**Actual**	**Budget**	**Variance**	**Variance %**	
9	**East**	87398	78950	8448	10.70044	
10	**New York**	34698	31790	2908	9.147531	
11	**Massachu**	14657	13500	1157	8.57037	

Select cell A3. Right click on East Sales query and select *Insert >> Slider*:

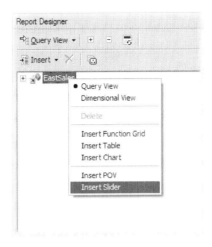

The Member Selection window will display. Choose the Product dimension (note the filter is set to *None* by default; all descendants of Product are displayed). Set the filter to Children. Select the children of Product:

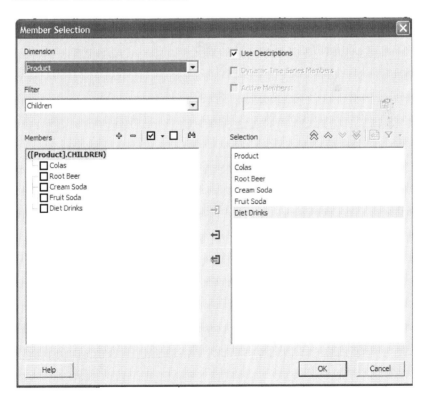

Click *OK*. The slider will insert into the spreadsheet:

	A	B	C	D	E	F	G	H
1	**Product Sales Report**							
2								
3								
4				Product - Product				
5								
6	East Region							
7								
8		Actual	Budget	Variance	Variance %			
9	East	87398	78950	8448	10.70044			
10	New York	34698	31790	2908	9.147531			
11	Massachu	14657	13500	1157	8.57037			
12	Florida	18341	16300	2041	12.52147			
13	Connectic	12411	10920	1491	13.65385			
14	New Ham	7291	6440	851	13.21429			
15								
16								
17								
18								
19		100000						
20								
21		80000						
22								
23		60000						

Move the slider to choose different products and note how the data is refreshed for the selected grids throughout the spreadsheet:

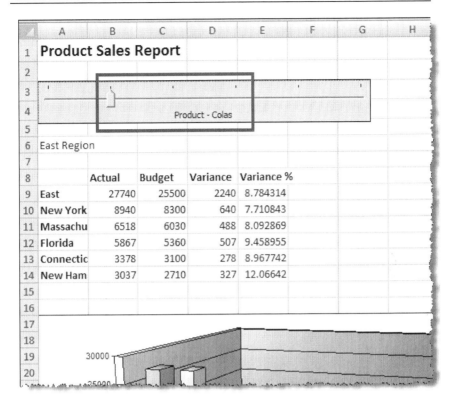

A new control called the POV control was added in the 11.1.1.1 release. We've changed our mind on the slider control and decided to use the new POV control instead.

Note! You can either use sliders or POV controls in a single query but not both.

To delete the slider control, expand the EastSales query by clicking the + sign. Click the + icon next to controls to view all the controls for the current query. Select *Slider 1* and click the delete icon (✕).

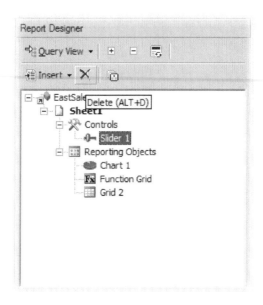

 Note! You can also delete reporting objects from a query like tables (a.k.a. Grids), function grids and charts.

Once the slider has been deleted, delete the empty rows (you won't need them as the POV is a floating object in the spreadsheet). Right click on the EastSales query and choose *Insert POV:*

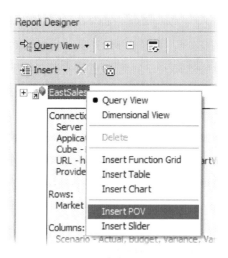

A floating POV is inserted into the report. Change the selections in the POV and your data will be refreshed to reflect the selection in all report objects:

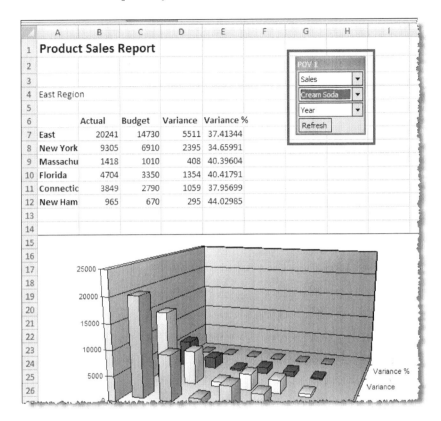

Congratulations, you've created your first report with the Report Designer. See what we mean about report creation on steroids? Save this as the Product Sales Report.xls and let's explore some additional features.

CREATE A REPORT WITH SUB QUERIES

You can use a smart slice in a report as we just saw, but what if you wanted to further modify the smart slice for specific member or filter selections? You can use a subquery to do so. Sub queries exist within report / workbook only (they are not available for other reports or users in the Data Source Manager).

In a blank spreadsheet, right click on the East Sales Smart slice. Select *Insert Subquery into Report*:

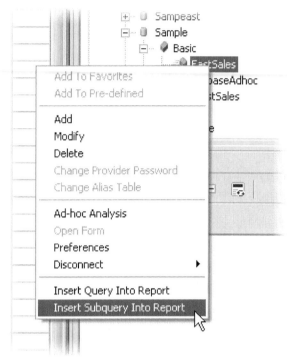

Choose the ellipses (...) for the Product dimension in the Design window:

Choose the Colas member:

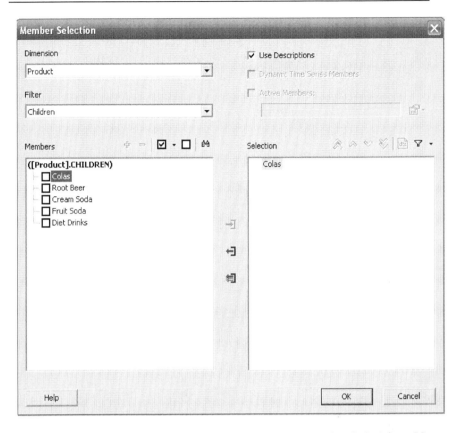

Click *OK*. Click the green arrow to process the definition. If desired, make any other changes to the smart slice selections. Click *OK*. Type in the new name for the subquery – *EastSales-Colas*:

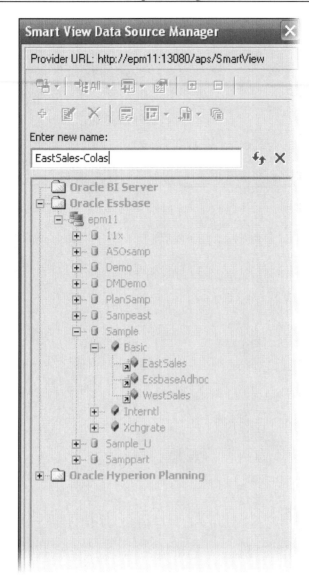

Click the *green revolving arrows* icon to save. Notice the subquery is inserted into the report designer but not saved as a smart slice:

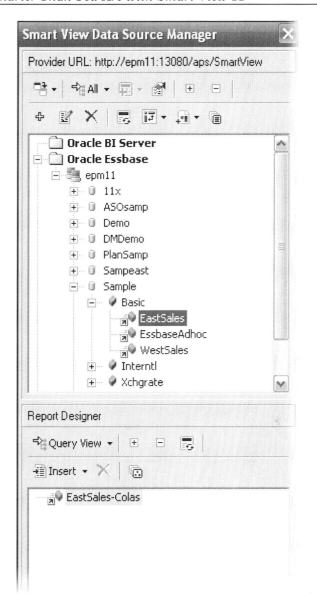

Try It!

Follow the same steps to create a subquery from East Sales for Root Beer called EastSales – RootBeer.

After you've created the two subqueries for Colas and Root Beer, insert each subquery into the blank worksheet by right clicking on it and selecting *Insert Function Grid*. Separate the grids with several rows and add a heading for each subquery:

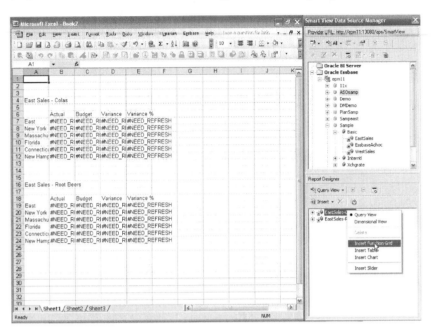

Now we want to insert a slider control to allow us to choose between the four quarters. To get us started, insert a few more rows at the beginning of the report (we want the slider to display at the top). Next, change the view from *Query View* to *Dimensional View*:

Note!   Query View shows Report Designer objects grouped by query. Dimensional View shows Report Designer objects by dimension. Dimensional view is important when you want to use the same dimension in a control for two different queries.

Select cell A1. Select Year in the Dimensional View window in the Report Designer. Right click on Year and select *Insert Slider*. Using the member selection window, choose the 4 quarters to display for the slider:

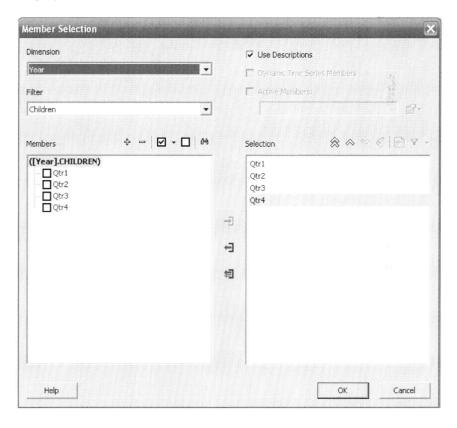

Click *OK* and notice the slider refreshes data for both grids:

	A	B	C	D	E	F	G	H	I	J	K
1	'						'				
2					Year - Qtr2						
3											
4	East Sales - Colas										
5											
6		Actual	Budget	Variance	Variance %						
7	East	7230	6760	470	6.952663						
8	New York	2358	2220	138	6.216216						
9	Massachu	1719	1620	99	6.111111						
10	Florida	1557	1450	107	7.37931						
11	Connecticu	799	750	49	6.533333						
12	New Hamp	797	720	77	10.69444						
13											
14											
15											
16	East Sales - Root Beers										
17											
18		Actual	Budget	Variance	Variance %						
19	East	5902	5650	252	4.460177						
20	New York	1989	1930	59	3.056995						
21	Massachu	1263	1210	53	4.380165						
22	Florida	1323	1260	63	5						
23	Connecticu	772	730	42	5.753425						
24	New Hamp	555	520	35	6.730769						

In order for a slider to work against multiple grids, the following rules must be met:

- Same dimension
- Same dimension definition (both grids must say "children of Year"; one cannot say children of Year and the other say descendants of Year)

Note! Note – the POV control is only available for a single grid.

Let's take this report a bit further to show you the possibilities. Add an Excel formula to calculate the total for Root Beer and Colas for all East regions. Apply formatting to the headers and data values:

	A	B	C	D	E	F
1						
2						
3			Year - Qtr2			
4	East Sales - Colas					
5						
6		Actual	Budget	Variance	Variance %	
7	East	$ 7,230	$ 6,760	$ 470	6.952663	
8	New York	$ 2,358	$ 2,220	$ 138	6.216216	
9	Massachusetts	$ 1,719	$ 1,620	$ 99	6.111111	
10	Florida	$ 1,557	$ 1,450	$ 107	7.37931	
11	Connecticut	$ 799	$ 750	$ 49	6.533333	
12	New Hampshire	$ 797	$ 720	$ 77	10.69444	
13						
14						
15						
16	East Sales - Root Beers					
17						
18		Actual	Budget	Variance	Variance %	
19	East	$ 5,902	$ 5,650	$ 252	4.460177	
20	New York	$ 1,989	$ 1,930	$ 59	3.056995	
21	Massachusetts	$ 1,263	$ 1,210	$ 53	4.380165	
22	Florida	$ 1,323	$ 1,260	$ 63	5	
23	Connecticut	$ 772	$ 730	$ 42	5.753425	
24	New Hampshire	$ 555	$ 520	$ 35	6.730769	
25						
26						
27	Colas & Root Beer Totals	$ 26,264	$ 24,820	$ 1,444	73.26861	
28						
29						

Now change the slider and note the formula and formatting are preserved. You're in love with Smart View now, aren't you? Us too. Save this report as EastSales-Detail.xls.

CASCADE WITH REPORT DESIGNER

Remember the totally awesome cool magician-like feature called Cascade (we realize we sound a bit silly with all the adjectives but we truly feel cascading is deserving of such a description). The one that generated a number of reports based on a list of members. Guess what? You can use Cascade on reports created with the Report Designer.

Open the Product Sales Report.xls spreadsheet. Delete the Product slider control by expanding the query EastSales, expanding *Controls* and delete the first slider (the Product slider that we created first):

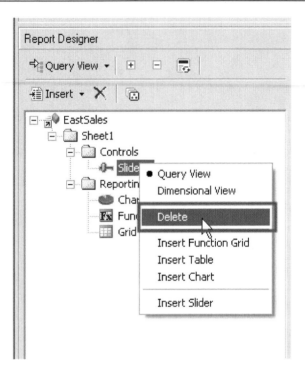

Click on the *Cascade Report Across the Workbook* icon in the Report Designer:

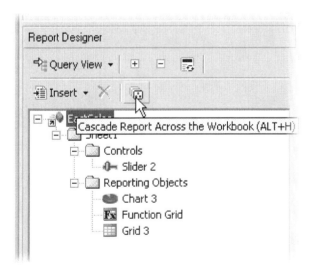

Don't click the Cascade for Adhoc Analysis.

Tip!

The Member Selection window will display. Choose the Product dimension and select the children of Product (we want a different report for each product category). Click *OK*:

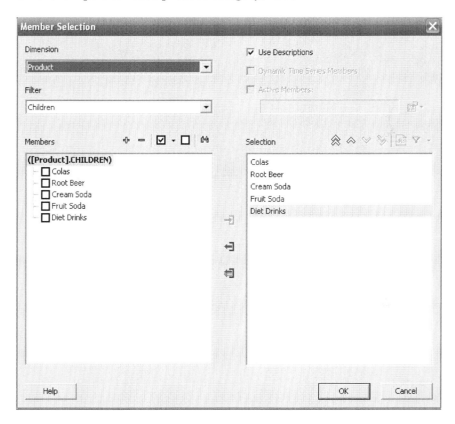

The different reports will generate (be amazed):

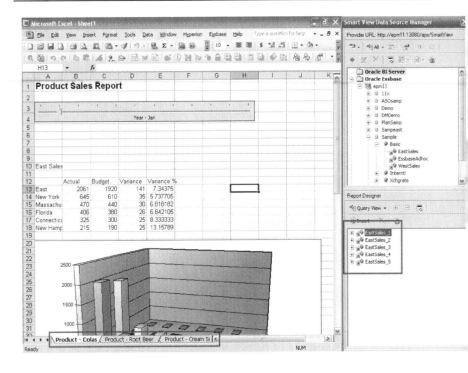

You may have to refresh the report by selecting *Refresh*.

Note!

New sub-queries are added in the Report Designer and each tab is named the member name or alias depending on your selection for the alias table.

Don't forget to format before cascading.

Tip!

CREATE A REPORT WITH REPORT DESIGNER IN WORD

As with all things Smart View, Smart Slices and Report Designer are available in Word and PowerPoint. Let's create a report with Report Designer in Word. Open a new Word document and in the Data Source Manager, connect to Sample.Basic. Click the

+ sign to expand Sample.Basic. Insert EastSales and WestSales smart slices into the Report Designer:

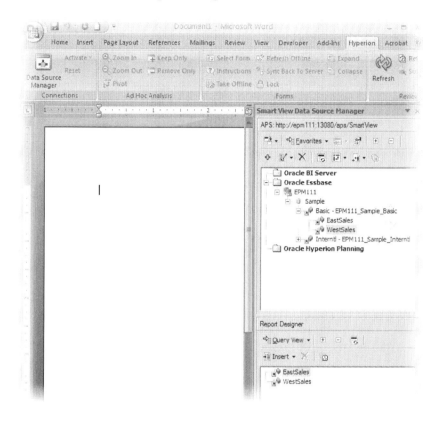

Next we need Select EastSales and select *Insert Function Grid* to place the grid in the Word document. Select *Refresh:*

	Actual	Budget	Variance	Variance %
East	87398	78950	8448	10.700443
New York	34698	31790	2908	9.147531
Massachusetts	14657	13500	1157	8.570370
Florida	18341	16300	2041	12.521472
Connecticut	12411	10920	1491	13.653846
New Hampshire	7291	6440	851	13.214286

Individual data points are inserted into a table in Word. You can now add table formatting and other font formatting as necessary. Although note in the example above, we're missing commas, dollar signs, etc. in the function grid.

 Remember that Smart Slice formatting options will not be applied in Report Designer.

Note!

If you manually add commas or $ to the function grid, they will be deleted upon refresh. There is really no good way to format numbers in a function grid in Word unfortunately. An alternative would be to copy and paste data points that have been formatted with Excel formatting. But this option doesn't use our handy Report Designer. What's the best answer (as of 11.1.1.)? If you really want to use the Report Designer and function grids, use Excel with Excel formatting to create the report and not Word.

 The POV Manager does not work with Report Designer objects (which makes sense; you should be using the POV control instead).

Note!

We've just inserted a function grid into a Word document. How about tables and charts? Sorry, no luck. These two objects are unavailable in Word documents. Cascade isn't supported in Word as well. But do these features work in PowerPoint? Let's next turn our attention to using Report Designer in PowerPoint and find out.

CASCADE A REPORT IN POWERPOINT

You should be a pro now in using the Report Designer. In a new PowerPoint document, connect to our old friend Sample.Basic. Insert the EastSales Smart Slice into the Report Designer (right click on the Smart Slice and select *Insert Query into Report*). Select EastSales query and select *Insert Function Grid*:

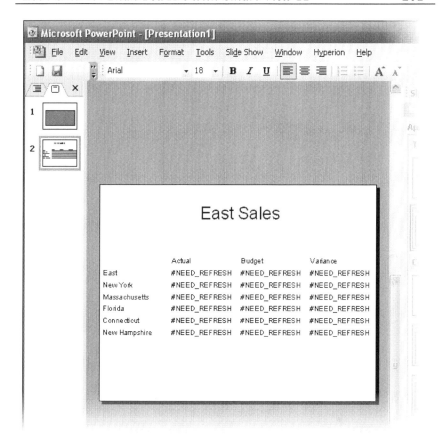

 Tip! You're grid may be sized a bit differently than above. Function grids are inserted as text boxes into PowerPoint where you can move, resize and align as needed (more on this in just a moment).

Click *Refresh* to retrieve the data. Now let's assume we are putting together a PowerPoint presentation with a slide on each product (level zero products). Do I have to go into each slide and insert the grid for each product? Of course not. Cascade to the rescue!

Click on the *Cascade* icon:

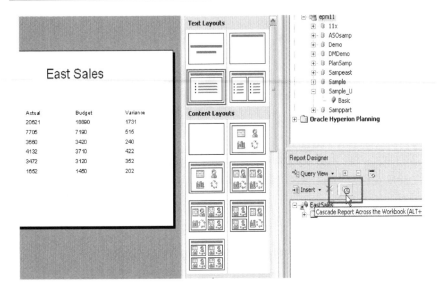

Choose the Product dimension and level zero products:

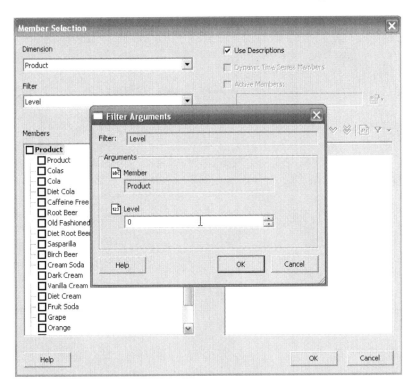

Change the Filter to Level and enter 0. Then click the *Check box* to select all the products at once:

Tip!

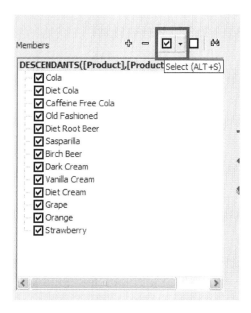

Click *OK* once the products have been selected. Wait a few seconds – note processing time will increase as the bursting member list increases. The report should display, one slide for each level zero product:

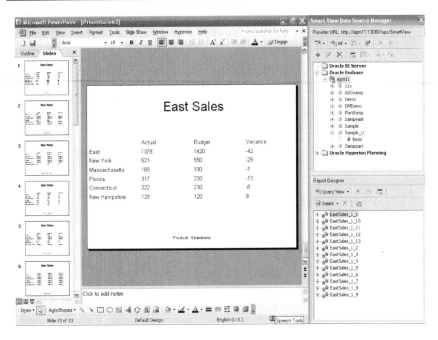

Wow. You just said that out loud, didn't you? Notice "footers" are automatically created identifying the cascaded member. And don't forget these are full refreshable data points. As the underlying data changes, you simply click *Refresh* or *Refresh All* to pull in the current data.

Does anyone see an issue with what we've done so far? We just cascaded an unformatted report. Now we have to go and reformat all of the slides individually. Lesson learned? Always finalize the formatting before we cascade (you don't want to have to recreate those TPS reports or worse, have Lumbergh remind you several times about the memo on formatting).

The same rules for formatting in Word apply in PowerPoint. You can't format the data points themselves. Any numeric formatting applied will be removed after refreshing the data. Tip - Manually add in text boxes with the $:

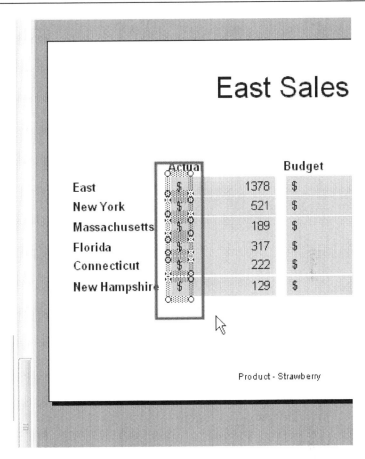

As you can see in our example, inserting the Function Grid actually inserts the data points as floating text boxes in the PowerPoint slide. You can format the text box background, border and font:

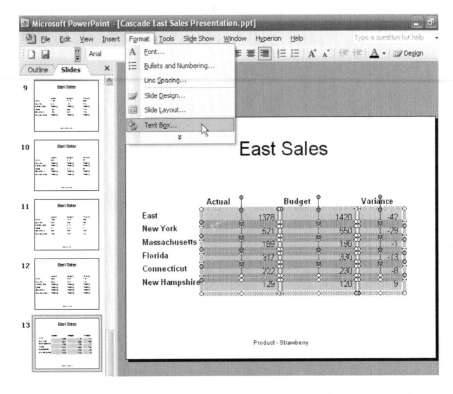

You can resize and reposition as necessary using PowerPoint features like alignment and distribution:

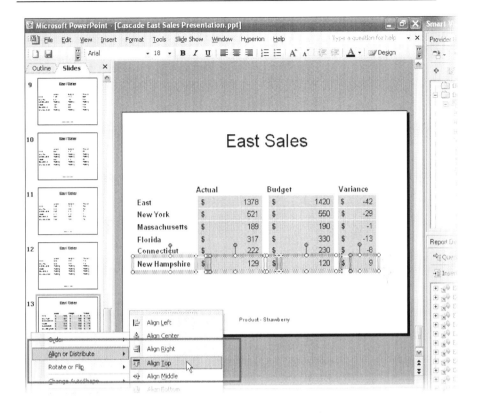

Apply formatting to the data points in our PowerPoint presentation. For example, format the color of the data point text boxes. Add in text boxes containing $.

Try It!

Insert a table and chart from the Report Designer into your PowerPoint presentation. Tables and charts are available!

Try It!

To fully view tables and charts in PowerPoint, you will need to switch to slideshow / presentation mode.

Tip!

Create a slide similar to the following, inserting the same Smart Slice query (EastSales) as a function grid, table and chart.:

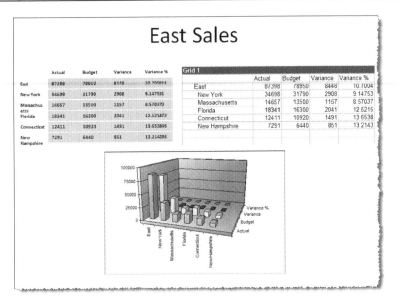

Notice the difference between the function grids (floating text boxes for each individual data point) vs. tables (single object with scroll bars). Instead of cascading this slide for all of the different products, let's add a POV control for selecting products dynamically for our upcoming meeting.

Right click on the slide (in our case Slide 2) and select *Insert POV*:

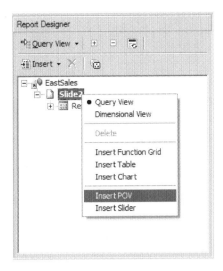

The POV Control is inserted into the slide as a grey box. Don't panic (like we did the first time we tried this) – in Normal PowerPoint mode, you won't be able to use the control:

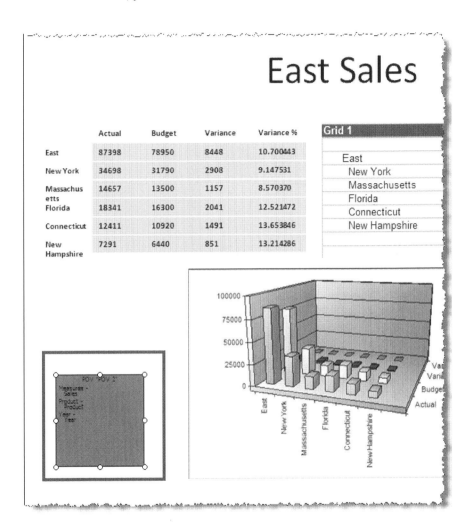

Change your mode to Slide Show / Presentation and you can to use the POV to select new POV members for the slide:

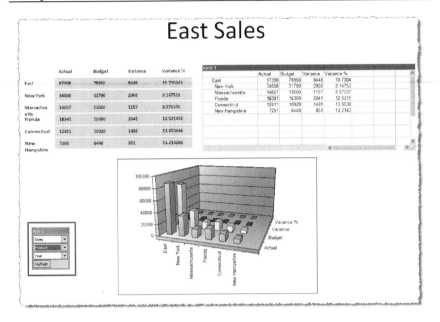

 The same grey box will appear after inserting slide controls as well. Never fear – switch to slide show / presentation mode and the slider becomes available for use.

Note!

 You can only use one control per query, either a slide or POV control. You cannot reuse the control on other slides for that query.

Note!

In summary, check out the following table to review what objects are available across multiple Office Products:

	Excel	*Word*	*PowerPoint*
Function Grid	Y	Y	Y
Table	Y	N	Y
Chart	Y	N	Y
Slider Control	Y	N	Y
POV Control	Y	N	Y

Congratulations! You did it. The interactive presentations, documents and spreadsheets that you created with Smart Slices and Report Designer knocked the socks off the consultants and executive management and left Lumbergh speechless. The dynamic session with live data resulted in the compliment for you "just a straight shooter with upper management written all over" from the consultants. And apparently Lumbergh had been laid off five years ago and was still getting a paycheck. Thank you to Essbase for helping to find this glitch. Now you are ready to conquer the world with value added reporting and analysis for your organization. You're almost to the end of the road but before we conclude the book, let's review some tips for creating fast retrieves and reports.

Chapter 7:
Speedy Retrieves

Now that you've mastered the majority of the Smart View Add-In menu items, we'll take your skills to the next level of mastery in a short but important chapter. It is not enough to simply understand how to retrieve and report data. Grasshopper, you must understand *why* data retrieves the way it does. One of the questions you must have been asking yourself at this point is "why do some retrieves take longer than others?"

Essbase retrieves are normally measured in seconds or subseconds. If your retrieves ever take more than thirty seconds, there are some things to check:

- Hardware performance.
- Retrieval size.
- Use of attribute dimensions.
- Use of dynamically calculated members.
- Use of dynamic time series.
- Dense vs. sparse retrievals.
- Essbase database settings.

Let's begin by assuming that your desktop, network, and Essbase server aren't older than dirt. If your hardware is more than a few years old, replace it, because doing so will definitely make things faster. Computers are easier to upgrade than people.

If your hardware is fairly recent, begin by looking at how much data you're retrieving. While 500 rows by 20 columns doesn't seem like much, that's over 10,000 cells of data you're asking Essbase to return. While you can't exactly eliminate every other row on your report to save space ("Sorry about the missing numbers, boss, but Edward Roske told me that deleting even numbered rows on my reports would cut my retrieval time in half!"), you'll at least be aware of why your report is taking a long time.

The next thing to review is your use of members from attribute dimensions, dynamically calculated members, and dynamic time series members. As mentioned earlier, all of these members are not pre-calculated. A retrieve that is accessing stored members will almost always run more quickly than one that accesses dynamic members.

One of the most common mistakes people make is putting the top member from an attribute dimension on their report. Notice the "Caffeinated" member on this retrieve:

A	B	C	D	E	F	
1		Market	Product	Actual	Caffeinated	
2	Qtr1	Qtr2	Qtr3	Qtr4	Year	
3 Sales	95,820	101,679	105,215	98,141	**400,855**	
4 COGS	42,877	45,362	47,343	43,754	**179,336**	
5 **Margin**	52,943	56,317	57,872	54,387	**221,519**	
6						
7 Marketing	15,839	16,716	17,522	16,160	**66,237**	
8 Payroll	12,168	12,243	12,168	12,168	**48,747**	
9 Misc	233	251	270	259	**1,013**	
10 **Total Expenses**	28,240	29,210	29,960	28,587	**115,997**	
11						
12 **Profit**	**24,703**	**27,107**	**27,912**	**25,800**	**105,522**	
13						

The presence of this member doesn't change the totals at all (we still have 105,522 in the bottom-right corner) but it takes a retrieve that would be against stored information and makes it entirely dynamic. Why? Because we are telling Essbase to go grab all the products that are Caffeinated_True and add them together, and then grab all the products that are Caffeinated_False and add them together, and finally, add Caffeinated_False to Caffeinated_True to get total Caffeinated. Well, this is the same value as if we'd never asked for Caffeinated at all!

The solution is obvious: delete the Caffeinated member and our retrieve will speed up by more than an order of magnitude. The more cynical among you might ask why Essbase isn't smart enough to notice that it's dynamically adding up every product when it could just take the stored Product total and be done with it. We don't have a good answer for that, so we'll pretend that we can't hear your question.

Dense vs. Sparse Retrievals

Density vs. Sparsity is a tricky subject, because it really gets in to how Essbase stores data behind the scenes and that's normally only of interest to an Essbase administrator, a developer, or a highly paid (but deservedly so) consultant. We're going to touch on the subject just enough so that you understand how it affects your retrieval times.

Our base dimensions (i.e., not the attribute dimensions) fall into one of two types: dense and sparse. Dense dimensions are dimensions for which most combinations are loaded with data. Sparse dimensions are often missing values.

In Sample.Basic, the dense dimensions are Year, Measures, and Scenario. This is because when there's a value for one month (say, Sales) there tends to be a value for every month. If there's a value for Sales, there tends to be a value for COGS, Marketing, and so on. If there's a number for Actual, there tends to be a value for Budget. As such, Year, Measures, and Scenario are said to be dense dimensions.

The sparse dimensions for Sample.Basic are Product and Market. This is because not every product tends to be sold in every state. As we saw earlier, out of seven possible caffeinated drinks, Massachusetts only sold three of them. As such, Product and Market are said to be sparse dimensions.

Why does this matter to you? Well, a retrieve consisting of dense dimensions (and only dense dimensions) in the rows and columns will tend to be much, much faster than a report with a sparse dimension in the rows or the columns.

When a report only has dense dimensions in the rows and columns, we refer to this as a dense retrieval. Here is an example of a dense retrieval against Sample.Basic:

	A	B	C	D	E
1		Product	Market	Scenario	
2		Jan	Feb	Mar	Apr	Ma
3	Sales	31,538	32,069	32,213	32,917	33
4	COGS	14,160	14,307	14,410	14,675	16
5	Margin	17,378	17,762	17,803	18,242	18
6	Marketing	5,223	5,289	5,327	5,421	5
7	Payroll	4,056	4,056	4,056	4,081	4
8	Misc	75	71	87	96	
9	Total Expenses	9,354	9,416	9,470	9,598	9
10	Profit	8,024	8,346	8,333	8,644	

It's a dense retrieval because Measures is in the rows, Year is in the columns, and both are dense dimensions. Notice that all the intersections tend to have values loaded to them. This is an example of a sparse retrieval against Sample.Basic:

	A	B	C	D	E	F
1		Jan	Sales	Actual		
2		New York	Massachusetts	Florida	Connecticut	New Hampshire Co
3	Cola	678	494	210	310	120
4	Diet Cola			200		
5	Caffeine Free Cola					93
6	Old Fashioned	61	126	190	180	90
7	Diet Root Beer			180	130	
8	Sasparilla					
9	Birch Beer	490	341			65
10	Dark Cream	483	130	120	190	76
11	Vanilla Cream	180		150	170	
12	Diet Cream			110		
13	Grape	234	80	80	123	45
14	Orange	219				
15	Strawberry	134	80	81	94	43

This is a sparse retrieval because Product is in the rows, Market is in the columns, and both are sparse dimensions. Notice that a number of the values are missing. Though it doesn't have many more cells to retrieve, this retrieval will take many times longer than the one above because of how Essbase retrieves data from sparse dimensions. Simply put, for sparse retrievals, Essbase retrieves a lot of data into memory on the server side that you'll never see or use.

While we can't change which dimensions are dense or sparse (that's a setting controlled for each database by the Essbase Administrator), we can be aware that sparse retrievals will take much longer than dense retrievals.

If you've tried all of the tips above and your retrieval is still taking a long time, it might be an issue with some of the database settings on the Essbase server. There are a number of settings such as density/sparsity (mentioned above), data caches, index caches, and so forth that someone qualified in Essbase can tune to improve retrieval performance. The bad news is that you can't tweak these yourself, but the good news is that they can be tweaked by someone else.

Chapter 8:
DIFFERENT APPLICATIONS

Everything we've done up to this point has been using the Sample.Basic database that comes with Essbase. While it's workable for exercises in this book, it's not terribly representative of databases in the real world. The goal for this chapter is to describe a few common types of databases in case you should ever run into them. For each application type, we'll review how the application is generally used and what the dimensions tend to be for that type of application. The most important take-away from this chapter: While Essbase is very good at financial analysis, it can support many, many different types of applications.

Note!

While an application can house one or more databases, most applications contain just one database. With that said, this chapter uses the terms "application" and "database" in the broader Information Technology sense.

COMMON DIMENSIONS

While every application will be different, most applications draw from a common set of dimension templates. The details within each dimension may change and the names of the dimensions may differ, but the same dimensions will keep appearing throughout many Essbase applications at your company. While we'll review later the differences for each specific application, it seems like a good idea to start with what we all have in common.

Time

All of us experience the constant effects of time and likewise (with very few exceptions), every Essbase database has one *or more* time dimensions. This is the dimension that contains the time periods for your database. Sample.Basic calls this dimension "Year":

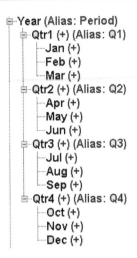

```
⊟ Year (Alias: Period)
  ⊟ Qtr1 (+) (Alias: Q1)
    ├ Jan (+)
    ├ Feb (+)
    └ Mar (+)
  ⊟ Qtr2 (+) (Alias: Q2)
    ├ Apr (+)
    ├ May (+)
    └ Jun (+)
  ⊟ Qtr3 (+) (Alias: Q3)
    ├ Jul (+)
    ├ Aug (+)
    └ Sep (+)
  ⊟ Qtr4 (+) (Alias: Q4)
    ├ Oct (+)
    ├ Nov (+)
    └ Dec (+)
```

In addition to Year, other common names for this dimension include Periods, All Periods, Time (my personal favorite), Time Periods, Full Year, Year Total, and History. As you can tell from the plus signs above next to each member, this dimension generally aggregates from the bottom-up.

A Time dimension will usually have one or more of the following generations:

- Years
  - Seasons
    - Halves
      - Quarters
        - Months
          - Weeks
            - Days

While it is not unheard of to have an application that looks at hours or portions of hours, this is normally split off into its own dimension and called something like "Hours" or "Time of Day." Call center analysis applications and some retail sales applications analyze data by portions of a day.

It is quite common for an Essbase application to have two time dimensions. One dimension will house the quarters, months, days, and so forth. A separate dimension, generally called "Years" or "FY" (for Fiscal Year), will contain the calendar year. Here's an example of a Years dimension:

⊟··Years (Alias: Current Year)
   ⊢ FY03 (~) (Alias: 2003)
   ⊢ FY04 (~) (Alias: 2004)
   ⊢ FY05 (~) (Alias: 2005)
   ⊢ FY06 (+) (Alias: 2006)
   ⊢ FY07 (~) (Alias: 2007)
   ⊢ FY08 (~) (Alias: 2008)
   ⊢ FY09 (~) (Alias: 2009)
   ⊢ FY10 (~) (Alias: 2010)

Unlike the Time dimensions that usually contain quarters and months, Years dimensions typically do not aggregate. Most often, the top member of a Years dimension is set to equal the data in the current year. In the above image, the tilde (~) signs (also called "no consolidate" tags) denote which years are not to be added into the total. As you can see, only FY06 has a plus next it, and therefore, is the only one to roll into Years. As such, Years equals FY06.

Some applications will combine a Time and Years dimension into one. This is often done when the Time dimension goes all the way down to the day-level and a company wants to do analysis by day of the week:

⊟·Time {Day of Week}
  ⊞··2005 (+)
  ⊞··2006 (+)
  ⊟·2007 (+)
    ⊞··Jan, 2007 (+)
    ⊞··Feb, 2007 (+)
    ⊞··Mar, 2007 (+)
    ⊞··Apr, 2007 (+)
    ⊞··May, 2007 (+)
    ⊟·Jun, 2007 (+)
      ⊢ Jun 1, 2007 (+) {Day of Week: Friday}
      ⊢ Jun 2, 2007 (+) {Day of Week: Saturday}
      ⊢ Jun 3, 2007 (+) {Day of Week: Sunday}
      ⊢ Jun 4, 2007 (+) {Day of Week: Monday}
      ⊢ Jun 5, 2007 (+) {Day of Week: Tuesday}
      ⊢ Jun 6, 2007 (+) {Day of Week: Wednesday}
      ⊢ Jun 7, 2007 (+) {Day of Week: Thursday}
      ⊢ Jun 8, 2007 (+) {Day of Week: Friday}
      ⊢ Jun 9, 2007 (+) {Day of Week: Saturday}
      ⊢ Jun 10, 2007 (+) {Day of Week: Sunday}
      ⊢ Jun 11, 2007 (+) {Day of Week: Monday}
      ⊢ Jun 12, 2007 (+) {Day of Week: Tuesday}
      ⊢ Jun 13, 2007 (+) {Day of Week: Wednesday}

Each date in the dimension has a "Day of Week" user-defined attribute (UDA) assigned to it. "Jun 1, 2007," for instance, has a "Day of Week" attribute of Friday. If we had the years in a separate dimension, we would have to declare every June 1st to be a Friday. While the people born on June 1st would absolutely love this, the calendar makers would not. As such, we have to put the year in to specify a specific date as being a specific day of the week. Here is the "Day of Week" attribute dimension that is used in conjunction with the dimension above:

```
⊟ Day of Week [Type: Text]
   ─Sunday
   ─Monday
   ─Tuesday
   ─Wednesday
   ─Thursday
   ─Friday
   └─Saturday
```

While most Time dimensions use Essbase Dynamic Time Series functionality to calculate year-to-date and quarter-to-date members, it's not uncommon to come across an older Essbase outline that has actual YTD and QTD members. Usually, there will be a member called YTD (and/or QTD) in the Time dimension that will have a child for each month. For January, the member would be called either "Jan YTD" or "YTD Jan." Here's an example of a Time dimension with stored YTD members:

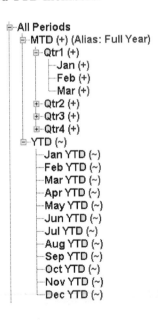

```
⊟ All Periods
   ⊟ MTD (+) (Alias: Full Year)
      ⊟ Qtr1 (+)
         ─Jan (+)
         ─Feb (+)
         └─Mar (+)
      ⊞ Qtr2 (+)
      ⊞ Qtr3 (+)
      ⊞ Qtr4 (+)
   ⊟ YTD (~)
      ─Jan YTD (~)
      ─Feb YTD (~)
      ─Mar YTD (~)
      ─Apr YTD (~)
      ─May YTD (~)
      ─Jun YTD (~)
      ─Jul YTD (~)
      ─Aug YTD (~)
      ─Sep YTD (~)
      ─Oct YTD (~)
      ─Nov YTD (~)
      └─Dec YTD (~)
```

Measures

Like Time, almost every Essbase application has a dimension that lists the metrics for the database. While common practice is to call this dimension Measures (as Sample.Basic does), other frequently used names include Accounts and Metrics.

In Sample.Basic, the Measures dimension contains some profit and loss accounts, inventory metrics, and three calculated ratios:

```
⊟ Measures
  ⊟ Profit (+)
    ⊟ Margin (+)
      ├ Sales (+)
      └ COGS (-)
    ⊟ Total Expenses (-)
      ├ Marketing (+)
      ├ Payroll (+)
      └ Misc (+)
  ⊟ Inventory (~)
    ├ Opening Inventory (+)
    ├ Additions (~)
    └ Ending Inventory (~)
  ⊟ Ratios (~)
    ├ Margin % (+)
    ├ Profit % (~)
    └ Profit per Ounce (~)
```

You'll notice that under "Profit," there are two members for "Margin" and "Total Expenses." Each one of these members has members below it. It's quite common for a Measures dimension to have many levels of hierarchy. A financial reporting application, for instance, might have hierarchy all the way down to a sub-account level.

While most every application will have a Measures dimension, what constitutes the Measures dimension will differ wildly:

- A financial reporting application will have accounts for income statement, balance sheet, and sometimes cash flow.
- An inventory analysis application will have measures for beginning inventory, ending inventory, additions, returns, adjustments, and so forth.
- A sales analysis application will have measures for sales dollars, units sold, and average sales price.

- A human capital analysis application will have metrics for payroll, FICA, FUTA, sick days, vacation days, years of employment, and so on.

The Measures dimension is the most important dimension in any application since it lets you define what metrics you're going to analyze, but you can safely expect every Measures dimension to be unique for every application.

It's worth pointing out that the Measures dimension in Sample.Basic is very odd. It's not normal to see inventory statistics along with profit and loss accounts in the same database. From what we can tell, this was only done to show in a sample database that Essbase can handle things beyond just financial metrics.

Scenario

This dimension is common to applications that in addition to actual data also have budget, forecast, or planning information. The "Scenario" dimension usually houses members such as Actual, Budget, Forecast, What-If, and several variances (differences between one scenario and another). While the most popular name for this dimension is Scenario (or Scenarios), other common names include Category, Ledger, Cases, and Versions.

As a general rule, we try to avoid calling my Scenario dimension "Versions," because Hyperion Planning also has a dimension called "Versions" in addition to a "Scenario" dimension. In Planning, the Versions dimension is used to differentiate between different drafts of budget and plan data. Members in a Versions dimension could be Initial, Draft 1, Draft 2, Draft 3, and Final. To avoid confusion in case you run across any lost Planning users at your company, don't name your Scenario dimension "Versions" when there are so many other good names from which to choose.

Here is Sample.Basic's Scenario dimension:

Most Scenario dimensions are non-aggregating (since it doesn't make a lot of sense to add Actual and Budget together). In Sample.Basic, the only child of Scenario to roll-up is Actual, in effect, setting Scenario equal to Actual.

```
⊟ Scenario
  ├ Actual (+)
  ├ Budget (~)
  ├ Variance (~)
  └ Variance % (~)
```

Other Dimensions

Many applications have a dimension that differentiates between different organizational entities. Commonly, this dimension is called Entities (the name Hyperion Planning prefers), Organization (the name we prefer), Departments, Cost Centers,

Companies, Locations, and other industry specific names (like Stores or Branches). The closest Sample.Basic has to an Organization dimension is the Market dimension.

Another common dimension that you might run across is Product which houses the relationships between products and their categories and families. This is one of the few dimensions where just about everyone calls it the same thing although the alias differs at the top of the dimension, containing something like "All Products" or "Total Products." The greatest difference in this dimension is the depth to which different applications go. Some Product dimensions stop at different classes of products while others will go all the way down to individual parts, items, or SKUs (Stock Keeping Units).

Other dimensions tend to be specific to different types of applications. For instance, a Customer dimension will tend to show up in Sales Analysis and Accounts Receivable applications. We'll cover some of the major applications you'll tend to see. This is by no means thorough, because every day, a company comes up with some new way to use Essbase that no one has ever tried before.

Please don't think that Essbase can only be used for financial applications. We once built an Essbase cube to track projects that families signed up for at our church Advent workshop. Okay, that's really geeky, but it goes to show you what you can do if you get out of the finance realm.

FINANCIAL REPORTING

Financial reporting (often called General Ledger, or GL analysis) databases are by far the most common type of Essbase application. This goes back to the early days of Essbase when the Arbor Software sales team used to sell pretty much exclusively into finance and accounting departments. Even today, the first Essbase database most companies build is to facilitate general ledger analysis.

In all fairness, Essbase is very good at doing GL analysis. Essbase has hundreds of built-in financial functions that make it a good fit for GL reporting. The Essbase outline provides a user friendly view of how accounts, departments, and other entities roll up within hierarchies and dimensions. It is also very easy for finance-minded personnel to manage those hierarchies. The most attractive thing about Essbase to accountants, though, is that accountants love Excel and as you just saw from the earlier chapters, Excel loves Essbase (or is that the other way around?).

Financial Reporting applications generally receive data from one or more GL Systems (including those that are part of a larger

ERP solution). Generally, this data is loaded monthly right after a financial close, but it is sometimes loaded more frequently during the close process.

Typical Financial Reporting dimensions include those common dimensions just discussed: Time, Measures, Scenario, Organization and Years. Measures will contain your account hierarchies for income statement, balance sheet, metrics, and cash flow. You can have alternate hierarchies to support different reporting requirements (more on that later).

In addition to the common dimensions, you will have those dimensions for which you'd like to perform analysis – by Geography, Product, Channel, or any other imaginable dimension that makes sense for your company. That's the beauty of Essbase: dimensionality is flexible and 100% customizable.

SALES ANALYSIS

Sales Analysis applications are a natural fit for Essbase, because they require fast retrievals at detailed levels. We once built a Sales Analysis application (sometimes called Flash Sales) that had data by store (for over 5,000 stores) by SKU (for over 100,000 products) by day for three years. It was an obscene amount of detail, but Essbase handled it flawlessly with retrievals measured in seconds.

Typical dimensions for this class of application such as Product, Location, and Geography. You can also view sales data by demographics like age and income level of buyer, by store information like store manager, square footage, store type, or location, or by product information like promotion or introduction date:

```
Income Level
  Under 20,000 (+)
  20,000-29,999 (+)      Payment Type
  30,000-49,999 (+)        Cash (+)
  50,000-69,999 (+)        ATM (+)
  70,000-99,999 (+)        Check (+)
  100,000 & Over (+)       Credit Card (+)
```

```
⊟ Age
  ⊟ Teens (+)
    ─ 1 to 13 Years (+)
    └ 14 to 19 Years (+)
  ⊟ Adults (+)
    ─ 20 to 25 Years (+)
    ─ 26 to 30 Years (+)
    ─ 31 to 35 Years (+)
    ─ 36 to 45 Years (+)
    └ 46 to 54 Years (+)
  ⊞ Senior (+)
```

Time dimensions will often go to the day level (and be tracked across multiple years) and have attributes for day of week. Measures or accounts will often include units sold, cost of goods sold, price, revenue, and much more. Some sales applications have inventory data as well and include weeks of supply calculations.

With the introduction of Aggregate Storage Option (known in System 9 as "Enterprise Analytics"), the level of detail that can be loaded into Sales Analysis applications has grown exponentially. The advent of 64-bit Essbase has expanded the size of some of these databases even further since 64-bit Essbase allows far more RAM to be allocated to individual Essbase applications.

Unlike financial reporting applications which are generally fed from GLs or ERPs, Sales Analysis applications are generally fed from data warehouses, operational data stores, and legacy systems. It is not uncommon for Sales Analysis databases to be loaded every night with the prior day's sales data.

HUMAN CAPITAL ANALYSIS

Human Capital Analysis applications allow companies to analyze one of their most important assets: their people. (How important are certain people in your organization? Discuss.) Sometimes these applications are called Human Resources analysis, Employee analysis, or Salary analysis. We'll go with "Human Capital" analysis because it's trendy. "Human Resources" is *so* five minutes ago.

In addition to the ubiquitous Measures and Time, common dimensions for Human Capital applications include employee, employee status, job grade, and function. Detailed applications could also include title, start dates, and other employee-level information. It's also not uncommon to have Equal Employment Opportunity Commission attributes such as race, gender, age, and veteran status.

The Measures dimension will have accounts that tend to map to the General Ledger (particularly, the payroll or compensation section of the income statement).

```
⊟ 501000 (+) (Alias: Total Compensation)
  ⊟ 501100 (+) (Alias: Salaries and Wages)
    ⊞ 501110 (+) (Alias: Total Salary)
    ⊞ 501120 (+) (Alias: Overtime)
      501130 (+) (Alias: Bonus Expense)
      501150 (+) (Alias: Auto Allowance)
  ⊞ 501200 (+) (Alias: Taxes and Benefits)
```

You can also use different drivers to budget and plan employee costs. Headcount, Start Month, Vacation Days, Sick Days, and many more can be used in calculations to complete accurate planning numbers.

These drivers can also provide invaluable insight into historical employee trends. We once knew a company that analyzed employee sick time patterns to find out which employees tended to be "sick" on Mondays more than any other day of the week. Apparently, the Monday morning flu was a big problem at their company.

CAPITAL EXPENDITURE ANALYSIS

Capital Expenditure applications (often abbreviated to "Cap Ex" and sometimes called Capital Equipment or Fixed Asset) are another frequent type of Essbase cube. Whether it is determining the rate of return on an investment or it is tracking capital equipment requests from your organization, you can implement a CapEx application to suit your company's needs. Dimensions include capital equipment item, equipment type, asset category, and asset life.

Here are some examples of capital equipment dimensions:

```
⊟ Category
    ⸺ Capacity (+)
    ⸺ Capability (+)
    ⸺ Cost Reduction (+)
    ⸺ Maintenance (+)
    ⸺ Market Opportunity (+)
    ⸺ Quality (+)
    ⸺ No Category (+)
⊟ Projects
    ⊟ All Projects (+)
        ⸺ Laser Weld (+)
        ⸺ Plasma R&D (+)
        ⸺ Networking (+)
        ⸺ BPM Implementation (+)
    ⸺ No Project (+)

⊟ Equip Type
    ⊟ All Equip Types (+)
        ⸺ Building (+)
        ⸺ Leasehold Improv (+)
        ⸺ Mfg Machinery (+)
        ⸺ Office Furniture (+)
        ⸺ Computer Equip (+)
        ⸺ New Software (+)
        ⸺ Auto (+)
    ⸺ No Equip Type (+)
```

The Account dimension for these applications usually contains a portion of your Balance Sheet:

```
⊟ BalanceSheet (~) (Alias: Balance Sheet)
    ⊟ 100000 (+) (Alias: Total Assets)
        ⊟ 150000 (+) (Alias: Fixed Assets)
            ⊟ 151000 (+) (Alias: Gross PPE)
                ⸺ 151100 (+) (Alias: Construction in Progress)
                ⸺ 151200 (+) (Alias: Land)
                ⸺ 151300 (+) (Alias: Buildings)
                ⸺ 151400 (+) (Alias: Leasehold Improvements)
                ⸺ 151500 (+) (Alias: Mfg Mach and Equip)
                ⸺ 151600 (+) (Alias: Office Furn and Fixtures)
                ⸺ 151700 (+) (Alias: Computer Equipment)
                ⸺ 151800 (+) (Alias: Computer Software)
                ⸺ 151900 (+) (Alias: Vehicles)
            ⸺ 152000 (+) (Alias: Accumulated Depreciation)
```

Other metrics that tend to show up in the Measures dimension include quantities, charges, months in service, asset life, and other drivers related to capital equipment.

Generally, CapEx applications are loaded from the Fixed Asset module from your ERP, but it is not uncommon for plan data for capital expenditures to be entered directly into Essbase (or via Hyperion Planning's Capital Expenditure model available in System 9.3).

BUDGETING, PLANNING, AND FORECASTING

With highly sophisticated write back capabilities, Essbase provides an excellent solution for budgeting, planning, and forecasting systems. Hyperion Planning was built on top of Essbase specifically to take advantage of Essbase's sublime ability to not only be used for reporting of data, but also multi-user submission of data.

Back in the days before Hyperion Planning was invented, many companies built Essbase cubes for budgeting purposes. They sent their data in via the Essbase Add-In and they were happy. Essbase security limited the dimensions and members for which data could be entered by users and calc scripts were used to calculate data if necessary.

If Essbase is perfect for budgeting, why was Planning created? The answer is simply due to the needs of planners and budgeters expanding beyond the abilities of Essbase. Modern forecasters require things like audit trails, integrated workflow, web-based data entry, and more. While Essbase can meet straight-forward budget needs, it doesn't have the built-in functionality that you get when you pay for Hyperion Planning.

Budgeting and forecasting applications written in Essbase (or built in Essbase via Hyperion Planning) will tend to look very similar to your reporting and analysis applications. For example, you may have a budgeting application to capture budget for income statement items, another application for capital equipment planning, and another application for salary planning. Though these applications will be similar to your reporting and analysis applications, they often do not contain the same level of detail. In general, budget data is not as granular as actual data.

In the example below, budget is captured at the reporting line level of Market while actual data is captured by GL account:

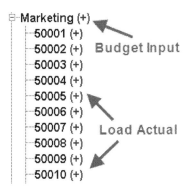

So...can we just capture budget and forecast information in my reporting and analysis applications? Yes, but there are some things to consider. First, understand the level of detail. If you are capturing budget at a higher level, you have to think carefully about how consolidations will take place in Essbase. If you enter data at an upper level and then run an aggregation, you could easily erase the data that was entered by users at the higher points in the dimension. There are ways to prevent this but the traditional work around is to use "dummy" members (see page below).

Second, we need to think about the dimensionality required for each purpose. In your reporting and analysis databases, you may want to analyze actual data by more dimensions or slices than you would for budget data. Too many dimensions can overly complicate the budgeting and planning process.

Third, you may also want to think about splitting reporting and budgeting for backup reasons. You'll want to backup your budgeting and planning applications more often as data changes far more frequently.

APPENDIX

Don't stop reading now. The Appendix has some helpful notes and knowledge to keep in your Smart View and Essbase toolbox.

NOTE ON THIS BOOK

Our objective is to teach you Smart View for Essbase data sources. Because Hyperion Planning stores data in Essbase, 100% of this book is applicable to Planning databases. About 75% of the content in this book is also applicable to analyzing and reporting against Financial Management sources. In version 11, Financial Management does not use the Common Provider Services and does not support Smart Slices and Report Designer.

We've tried to be as detailed as possible but if we described every single click or button, you'd be 100 years old before you were ready to use Essbase (and at that point, Hyperion would probably not even be an independent company but rather bought by some totally awesome firm like Oracle and Hyperion's CEO would be replaced with a really great guy like Larry Ellison, who if he's looking for an heir apparent should contact me at eroske@interrel.com). So we don't mention the fairly obvious tasks and buttons. For example, if there is a Close button, we probably skipped defining what this button does. Cancel means Cancel (doesn't save anything that you just did). Nothing tricky there.

NOTE ON SMART VIEW VERSIONS

Smart View was introduced pre-System 9 for Essbase but it wasn't the full product we know and love. The full product was introduced in System 9 though it has changed through the different versions 9.0 to 9.2, 9.3 and finally, 11x. While we love Smart View, various features will work in certain versions but not necessarily in other versions. The steps to perform tasks may also change (for example, in Smart View 9.2, you used Smart Tags to incorporate Essbase data in Word and PowerPoint and you use data points in 9.3). This book is based on version 11. So if I'm on 9.3, is this book applicable? It is actually with a few exceptions. Check out the later sections on Smart View 9.3.1.

WHY IS THIS OPTION GREYED OUT?

Smart View is the single add in for all of the Oracle EPM System and BI products. With that said, a number of options are specific to a product like Planning or Financial Management and are not available for Essbase connections. The common confusion culprits: Use Descriptions and Cell Text. These two Smart View features while seemingly applicable to Essbase are not available to Essbase: they are used for other products. The best place to look to figure out if a feature is available for your connection is the Smart View User guide (available on line). Check out the section called Features and Data Source Providers:

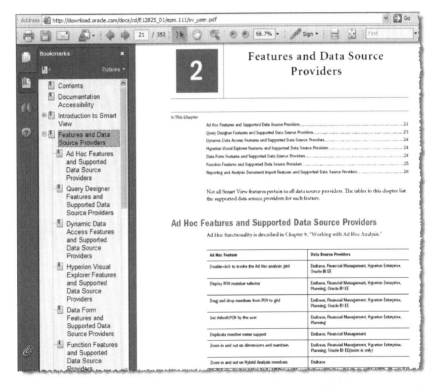

Helpful links (at the time of this publication in January 2009):

- http://download.oracle.com/docs/cd/E12825_01/epm.111/sv_u ser.pdf
- http://www.oracle.com/technology/documentation/epm.html

EXCEL ADD-IN VS. SMART VIEW ADD-IN 11.1.1.1

	Excel Add-in 11.1.1	*Smart View Add-in – Essbase 11.1.1.1*
Drill Capabilities	Yes	Yes
Keep only, Remove Only	Yes	Yes
Member Selection	Yes	Yes
Member Selection Filtering Options	Yes	Yes
Find in Member Selection	Yes	Yes
Advanced Member Selection by Subsets using Wildcards	Yes	No
Query Designer	Yes	Yes (different)
Suppress Missing Rows	Yes	Yes
Suppress Missing Columns	Yes	No
Retain Formulas	Yes (must select formula preservation)	Yes (by default)
Formula Fill on Zooms	Yes	No
Formula Fill on POV Change	Yes	Yes
Formatted Reports	Yes	Yes
Cell Text / LROs	Yes	No
Adjust function	No	Yes
DTS	Yes	Yes
Substitution Variables	Yes	**Yes**
Member name referenced in a linked formula	Yes	No; Coming Soon
Cascade	Yes	**Yes**

Ancestor Position	Yes	Yes
Use Excel Formatting & Cell Styles	Yes	Yes
Flashback / Undo	Yes – One Undo	Yes – Multiple Undo's
View Connection Information	*Options >> Styles tab*	Not as easily found
POV Manager – Copy and Paste POVs	No	Yes
Share POVs	No	Yes
Define Default Starting POV	No	**Yes with Smart Slices**
Multi-Source Grids / Reports	Yes	Yes (using data points)
Alias Table defaults to Default	Yes	No
Alias Table Selection Remembered through Session	Yes	No
Submit Data to Essbase	Yes	Yes
MDX vs. Rpt Script	Rpt Script	MDX
Copy / Paste Data Points	No	Yes
Visualize in Excel	No	Yes
Launch business rules	No	No

EXCEL ADD-IN VS. SMART VIEW ADD-IN 9.3.1

	Excel Add-in 9.3.1	*Smart View Add-in – Essbase 9.3.1*
Drill Capabilities	Yes	Yes
Keep only, Remove Only	Yes	Yes

Member Selection	Yes	Yes
Query Designer	Yes	Yes (different)
Retain Formulas	Yes (must select formula preservation)	Yes (by default)
Formatted Reports	Yes	Yes
Cell Text / LROs	Yes	No
Adjust function	No	Yes
DTS	Yes	Yes
Substitution Variables	Yes	No; Coming Soon
Member name referenced in a linked formula	Yes	No; Coming Soon
Cascade	Yes	No; Coming Soon
Ancestor Position	Yes	Yes
Use Excel Formatting & Cell Styles	Yes	Yes
Flashback / Undo	Yes – One Undo	Yes – Multiple Undo's
POV Manager – Copy and Paste POVs	No	Yes
Share POVs	No	Yes
Define Default Starting POV	No	No; Coming soon with Smart Slices
Multi-Source Grids / Reports	Yes	Yes (using data points)
Alias Table defaults to Default	Yes	No
Submit Data to Essbase	Yes	Yes
MDX vs. Rpt Script	Rpt Script	MDX
Copy / Paste Data Points	No	Yes
Visualize in Excel	No	Yes
Launch business rules	No	No

YOU HAVE BOTH EXCEL ADD-IN & SMART VIEW

...read this section.

Turn off Essbase

While those who use Essbase regularly love the mouse shortcuts, some people don't like Essbase turning off traditional Excel shortcuts. With Essbase mouse actions turned on, right-clicking on a cell does not bring up a context menu (with things like cut, copy, paste) and double-clicking on a cell does not allow in-cell editing.

To enable Excel actions, select *Essbase >> Options* and choose the Global tab:

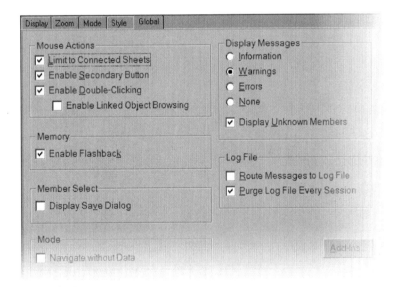

Uncheck *Enable Secondary Button* and *Enable Double-Clicking* and you'll be back to the Excel mousing you're used to. If you're curious why it says "Secondary" button instead of "Right" mouse button, it's so as not to offend left-handed people who have switched their mouse buttons. While it's nice not to offend the lefties, it confuses the heck out of the righties. For our purposes, secondary generally means "right."

There are some cases where you want to use the Essbase shortcuts but only when you're ready to retrieve data from Essbase.

To enable Essbase shortcuts on sheets that are currently connected to Essbase (i.e., sheets on which you've already chosen *Essbase >> Connect*), check the box for *Limit to Connected Sheets*.

If you install both the Essbase Add-In and the Smart View Add-In, you'll have two menu items in Excel. Here's a glimpse at the two menus:

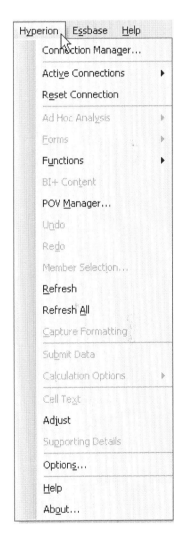

QUICK QUIDE TO SMART VIEW MENUS

Icon / Menu Option	Description
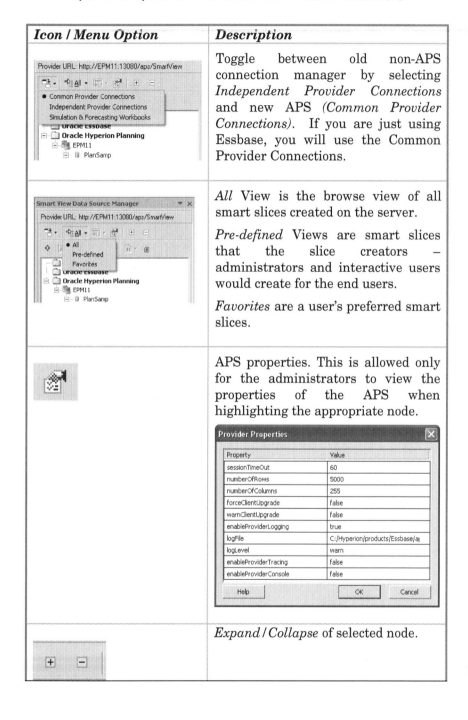	Toggle between old non-APS connection manager by selecting *Independent Provider Connections* and new APS *(Common Provider Connections)*. If you are just using Essbase, you will use the Common Provider Connections.
	All View is the browse view of all smart slices created on the server. *Pre-defined* Views are smart slices that the slice creators – administrators and interactive users would create for the end users. *Favorites* are a user's preferred smart slices.
	APS properties. This is allowed only for the administrators to view the properties of the APS when highlighting the appropriate node.
	Expand / Collapse of selected node.

Icon / Menu Option	Description
✛	*Add* - used to add either new servers or slices.
▣✎	*Modify* - used to edit servers or slice queries.
✕	*Delete* - button used to delete servers, apps, or smart slices.
▣↻	*Sync with Smart Slice* - used to find and sync with the view that created the selected query
▣▾ Ad-hoc Analysis Open Form	*Start Ad-Hoc / Open Form* - Open forms in ad-hoc mode or as forms.
▣▾ Query Subquery	*Insert into Report* - Insert queries or sub queries into a reporting framework.
▣	*Cascade Ad-Hoc Grid* - Used to create a cascade of ad-hoc view

YOU ARE ON SMART VIEW VERSION 9.3.1

If you are currently on Smart View 9.3.1, most of this book will still be applicable to you. Some of the 11.1.1.1 features will not be available to you like the Data Source Manager, Smart Slices, Report Designer, Cascade, etc but the remaining features work the same.

The main difference that we should cover with you related to 9.3.1 is how you connect in version 9.3.1 (a pretty different process from 11). Before you can perform analysis using Smart View, you must first specify the database for which you want to connect. You will use the Database Connection Manager to do this. Ready? Begin.

Connect to an Existing Database Connection

1. In Excel, select *Hyperion >> Connection Manager* or click the *Connect* button:

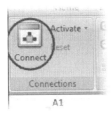

A list of the existing database connections will display in the Connection Manager:

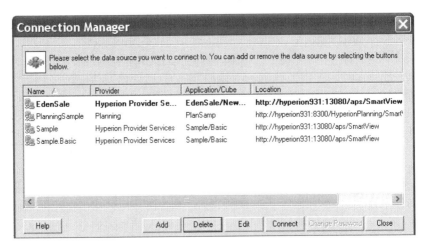

You can't help but notice that Smart View has a number of different types of database connections (the same ones we reviewed earlier in the book, some with different names):

*   Hyperion Provider Services (known as Analytic Services Smart View Provider in versions prior to 9.3) – Use this provider to perform analysis against an Essbase database (e.g. swap rows and columns, drill down, etc.).

- Financial Management Provider – Use this provider to connect to and perform Financial Management tasks.
- Hyperion Reporting and Analysis Provider (formerly known as Hyperion Smart View Provider for System 9 BI+) – Use this provider to import Financial Reporting, Web Analysis, Interactive Reporting, or Production Reporting documents into Microsoft Office applications.
- Planning Provider – Use this provider to export Planning web forms and enter Planning data.

2. Select one of the Hyperion Provider Services connections and click the *Connect* button.
3. Enter the user name and password.
4. Click *Connect*.
5. Click *Close* to close the Connection Manager.

View or Change Active Connections

1. Select *Hyperion >> Active Connections* or select the active connection from the drop down:

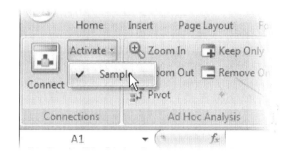

 After you connect to a data source, you must activate the source.

Tip!

Add a Database Connection via URL

The first time you use Smart View to connect to a database, you will need to create a new database connection.

1. In Excel, select *Hyperion >> Connection Manager* or click the *Connect* button:
2. The Connection Manager will display.
3. Click the *Add* button.

There are two ways to add Database Connections: Registered Shared Services application and direct connection using a URL.

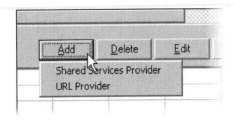

To use a direct connection via URL,
4. Select URL provider from the dropdown.
5. Select Hyperion Provider for Essbase connections.
6. Enter the location URL:

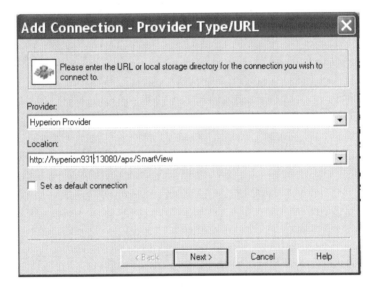

For Analytic Services (Essbase), the default location URL for version 9.3.1 is:

http(s):/ / <servername>:13080 / aps / SmartView

Check the Hyperion documentation to confirm the URLs for your version (yes, the URLS may differ between System 9 versions).

7. Optionally, you can specify this connection to be the default connection. Click *Next* and the database repository window will display.

8. Select the desired Essbase server.
9. Enter a valid Essbase user name and password:

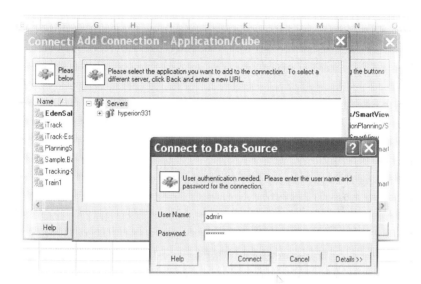

10. Click *Connect* and a list of the Essbase applications and databases will display.
11. Select Sample.Basic:

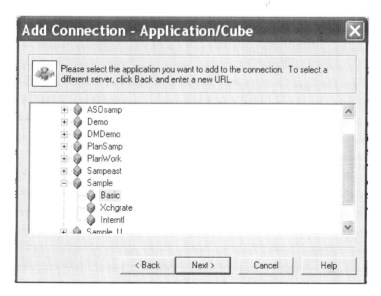

12. Click *Next*.

13. Enter a name and description for the database connection:

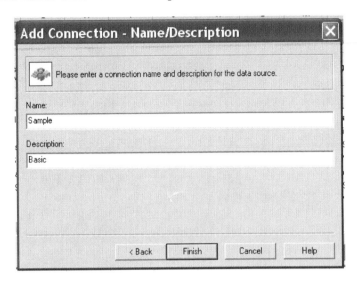

14. Click *Finish*.
15. The new database connection will now be listed in the Connection Manager. Select the Connection and click *Connect*:

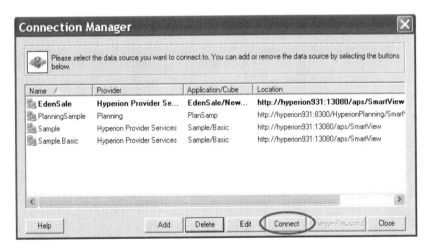

16. Click *Close* to close the Connection Manager.

Add a Database Connection via Shared Services

You will follow the same initial steps to create a database connection using the Shared Services Provider.

1. In Excel, select *Hyperion >> Connection Manager.*
2. The Connection Manager will display.
3. Click the *Add* button and select Shared Services:

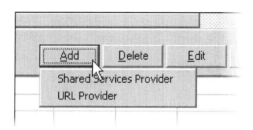

4. The Connection window will display. Verify the Shared Services URL:

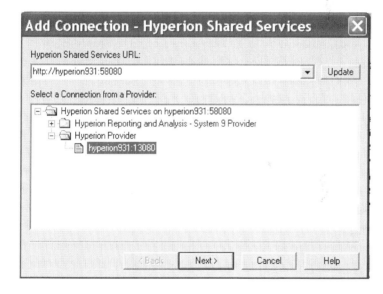

5. Click *Update* and a list of available providers in Shared Services will display.
6. Select the Essbase Server.
7. Click *Next.*

The remaining steps are the same as steps 8-16 of the URL database connection steps.

 Why should you use a Shared Services database connection versus a direct URL database connection?

Tip! Shared Services will store the provider URLs for all Hyperion products in one place (so you don't have to know each individual URL for each product; you only need to know the Shared Services connection information).

Use the Connection Manager to edit and then delete the connection you just added.

Try It!

Once you have added the database connection, you may want to assign the alias table for the connection. Doesn't Smart View default to the default alias table? While that would make sense, the current versions of Smart View does not default to the default alias table. To define the alias table for the connection, right click on the database connection and select *Change Alias Table*:

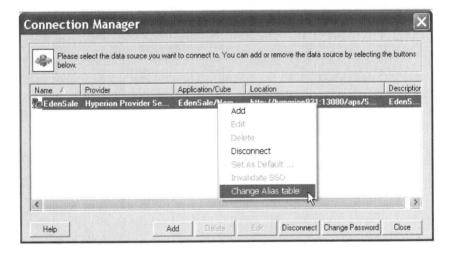

The available alias tables will display. Choose the desired alias table and click *OK*:

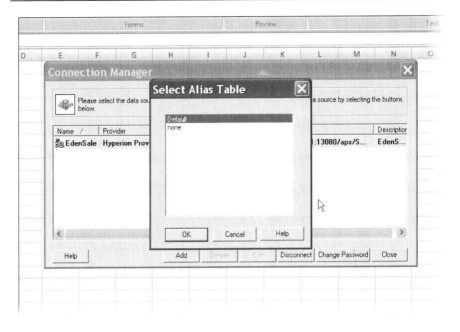

INDEX

34644421R00162

Made in the USA
Lexington, KY
16 August 2014